The Life of St. Anthony

By St. Athanasius

Henderson Publishing

The Life of St. Anthony translated by H. Ellershaw, in *Select Writings and Letters of Athanasius*, edited by Archibald Robertson; volume 4 of The Nicene and Post-Nicene Fathers, second series, edited by Philip Schaff.

Published May 2024.
Version: 2.0.
ISBN: 978-1-964170-20-6.

If you have a question or have found an error concerning this manuscript, please email: contact@hendersonpublishing.com

Book cover designed by Christian Caudill.
Book designed by Jeremy Hausotter.
Front cover image: The Destruction of Leviathan by Gustav Doré. Wikimedia Commons.

This book has been typeset in Garamond Libre.

Henderson Publishing | San Antonio, Texas

Table of Contents

The Life of St. Anthony

The life and conversation of our holy Father, Antony: written and sent to the monks in foreign parts by our Father among the Saints, Athanasius, Bishop of Alexandria.

Athanasius the bishop to the brethren in foreign parts.

Preface

OU HAVE ENTERED upon a noble rivalry with the monks of Egypt by your determination either to equal or surpass them in your training in the way of virtue. For by this time there are monasteries among you, and the name of monk receives public recognition. With reason, therefore, all men will approve this determination, and in answer to your prayers God will give its fulfilment. Now since you asked me to give you an account of the blessed Antony's way of life, and are wishful to learn how he began the discipline, who and what manner of man he was previous to this, how he closed his life, and whether the things told of him are true, that you also may bring yourselves to imitate him, I very readily accepted your behest, for to me also the bare recollection of Antony is a great accession of help.

1

And I know that you, when you have heard, apart from your admiration of the man, will be wishful to emulate his determination; seeing that for monks the life of Antony is a sufficient pattern of discipline. Wherefore do not refuse credence to what you have heard from those who brought tidings of him; but think rather that they have told you only a few things, for at all events they scarcely can have given circumstances of so great import in any detail. And because I at your request have called to mind a few circumstances about him, and shall send as much as I can tell in a letter, do not neglect to question those who sail from here: for possibly when all have told their tale, the account will hardly be in proportion to his merits. On account of this I was desirous, when I received your letter, to send for certain of the monks, those especially who were wont to be more frequently with him, that if I could learn any fresh details I might send them to you. But since the season for sailing was coming to an end and the letter-carrier urgent, I hastened to write to your piety what I myself know, having seen him many times, and what I was able to learn from him, for I was his attendant for a long time, and poured water on his hands; (cf. 2 Kings 3:11) in all points being mindful of the truth, that no one should disbelieve through hearing too much, nor on the other hand by hearing too little should despise the man.

Birth and beginnings of Antony

1. Antony you must know was by descent an Egyptian: his parents were of good family and possessed considerable wealth, and as they were Christians he also was reared in the same Faith. In infancy he was brought up with his parents, knowing nought

else but them and his home. But when he was grown and arrived at boyhood, and was advancing in years, he could not endure to learn letters, not caring to associate with other boys; but all his desire was, as it is written of Jacob, to live a plain man at home. (Genesis 25:27.) With his parents he used to attend the Lord's House, and neither as a child was he idle nor when older did he despise them; but was both obedient to his father and mother and attentive to what was read, keeping in his heart what was profitable in what he heard. And though as a child brought up in moderate affluence, he did not trouble his parents for varied or luxurious fare, nor was this a source of pleasure to him; but was content simply with what he found nor sought anything further.

2. After the death of his father and mother he was left alone with one little sister: his age was about eighteen or twenty, and on him the care both of home and sister rested. Now it was not six months after the death of his parents, and going according to custom into the Lord's House, he communed with himself and reflected as he walked how the Apostles left all and followed the Saviour; (Matthew 4:20) and how they in the Acts (Acts 4:35) sold their possessions and brought and laid them at the Apostles' feet for distribution to the needy, and what and how great a hope was laid up for them in heaven. Pondering over these things he entered the church, and it happened the Gospel was being read, and he heard the Lord saying to the rich man, "If you would be perfect, go and sell that you have and give to the poor; and come follow Me and you shall have treasure in heaven." (Matthew 19:21) Antony, as though God had put him in mind of the Saints, and the passage had been read on his account, went out immediately

from the church, and gave the possessions of his forefathers to the villagers—they were three hundred acres, productive and very fair—that they should be no more a clog upon himself and his sister. And all the rest that was movable he sold, and having got together much money he gave it to the poor, reserving a little however for his sister's sake.

His early ascetic life

3. And again as he went into the church, hearing the Lord say in the Gospel, "be not anxious for the morrow," (Matthew 6:34) he could stay no longer, but went out and gave those things also to the poor. Having committed his sister to known and faithful virgins, and put her into a convent to be brought up, he henceforth devoted himself outside his house to discipline, taking heed to himself and training himself with patience. For there were not yet so many monasteries in Egypt, and no monk at all knew of the distant desert; but all who wished to give heed to themselves practised the discipline in solitude near their own village. Now there was then in the next village an old man who had lived the life of a hermit from his youth up. Antony, after he had seen this man, imitated him in piety. And at first he began to abide in places outside the village: then if he heard of a good man anywhere, like the prudent bee, he went forth and sought him, nor turned back to his own palace until he had seen him; and he returned, having got from the good man as it were supplies for his journey in the way of virtue. So dwelling there at first, he confirmed his purpose not to return to the abode of his fathers nor to the remembrance of his kinsfolk; but to keep all his desire and energy for perfecting his discipline. He worked, however,

with his hands, having heard, "he who is idle let him not eat," (2 Thessalonians 3:10) and part he spent on bread and part he gave to the needy. And he was constant in prayer, knowing that a man ought to pray in secret unceasingly. (Matthew 6:7; 1 Thessalonians 5:17.) For he had given such heed to what was read that none of the things that were written fell from him to the ground, but he remembered all, and afterwards his memory served him for books.

4. Thus conducting himself, Antony was beloved by all. He subjected himself in sincerity to the good men whom he visited, and learned thoroughly where each surpassed him in zeal and discipline. He observed the graciousness of one; the unceasing prayer of another; he took knowledge of another's freedom from anger and another's loving-kindness; he gave heed to one as he watched, to another as he studied; one he admired for his endurance, another for his fasting and sleeping on the ground; the meekness of one and the long-suffering of another he watched with care, while he took note of the piety towards Christ and the mutual love which animated all. Thus filled, he returned to his own place of discipline, and henceforth would strive to unite the qualities of each, and was eager to show in himself the virtues of all. With others of the same age he had no rivalry; save this only, that he should not be second to them in higher things. And this he did so as to hurt the feelings of nobody, but made them rejoice over him. So all they of that village and the good men in whose intimacy he was, when they saw that he was a man of this sort, used to call him God-beloved. And some welcomed him as a son, others as a brother.

Early conflicts with the devil

5. But the devil, who hates and envies what is good, could not
endure to see such a resolution in a youth, but endeavoured to
carry out against him what he had been wont to effect against
others. First of all he tried to lead him away from the discipline,
whispering to him the remembrance of his wealth, care for his
sister, claims of kindred, love of money, love of glory, the various
pleasures of the table and the other relaxations of life, and at last
the difficulty of virtue and the labour of it; he suggested also the
infirmity of the body and the length of the time. In a word he
raised in his mind a great dust of debate, wishing to debar him
from his settled purpose. But when the enemy saw himself to
be too weak for Antony's determination, and that he rather was
conquered by the other's firmness, overthrown by his great faith
and falling through his constant prayers, then at length putting
his trust in the weapons which are "in the navel of his belly"
(Job 40:16) and boasting in them—for they are his first snare for
the young—he attacked the young man, disturbing him by night
and harassing him by day, so that even the onlookers saw the
struggle which was going on between them. The one would
suggest foul thoughts and the other counter them with prayers:
the one fire him with lust, the other, as one who seemed to blush,
fortify his body with faith, prayers, and fasting. And the devil,
unhappy wight, one night even took upon him the shape of a
woman and imitated all her acts simply to beguile Antony. But he,
his mind filled with Christ and the nobility inspired by Him, and
considering the spirituality of the soul, quenched the coal of the
other's deceit. Again the enemy suggested the ease of pleasure.

But he like a man filled with rage and grief turned his thoughts to the threatened fire and the gnawing worm, and setting these in array against his adversary, passed through the temptation unscathed. All this was a source of shame to his foe. For he, deeming himself like God, was now mocked by a young man; and he who boasted himself against flesh and blood was being put to flight by a man in the flesh. For the Lord was working with Antony—the Lord who for our sake took flesh and gave the body victory over the devil, so that all who truly fight can say, "not I but the grace of God which was with me." (1 Corinthians 15:10.)

6. At last when the dragon could not even thus overthrow Antony, but saw himself thrust out of his heart, gnashing his teeth as it is written, and as it were beside himself, he appeared to Antony like a black boy, taking a visible shape in accordance with the color of his mind. And cringing to him, as it were, he plied him with thoughts no longer, for guileful as he was, he had been worsted, but at last spoke in human voice and said, "Many I deceived, many I cast down; but now attacking you and your labours as I had many others, I proved weak." When Antony asked, Who are you who speak thus with me? He answered with a lamentable voice, "I am the friend of whoredom, and have taken upon me incitements which lead to it against the young. I am called the spirit of lust. How many have I deceived who wished to live soberly, how many are the chaste whom by my incitements I have over-persuaded! I am he on account of whom also the prophet reproves those who have fallen, saying, 'You have been caused to err by the spirit of whoredom.' (Hosea 4:12.) For by me they have been tripped up. I am he who have so often troubled

you and have so often been overthrown by you." But Antony having given thanks to the Lord, with good courage said to him, "You are very despicable then, for you are black-hearted and weak as a child. Henceforth I shall have no trouble from you, for 'the Lord is my helper, and I shall look down on mine enemies.' " (Psalm 118:7.) Having heard this, the black one straightway fled, shuddering at the words and dreading any longer even to come near the man.

Details of his life at this time (271-285?)

7. This was Antony's first struggle against the devil, or rather this victory was the Saviour's work in Antony, "Who condemned sin in the flesh that the ordinance of the law might be fulfilled in us who walk not after the flesh but after the spirit." (Romans 8:3-4.) But neither did Antony, although the evil one had fallen, henceforth relax his care and despise him; nor did the enemy as though conquered cease to lay snares for him. For again he went round as a lion seeking some occasion against him. But Antony having learned from the Scriptures that the devices of the devil are many, (Ephesians 6:11) zealously continued the discipline, reckoning that though the devil had not been able to deceive his heart by bodily pleasure, he would endeavour to ensnare him by other means. For the demon loves sin. Wherefore more and more he repressed the body and kept it in subjection, (1 Corinthians 9:27) lest haply having conquered on one side, he should be dragged down on the other. He therefore planned to accustom himself to a severer mode of life. And many marvelled, but he himself used to bear the labour easily; for the eagerness of soul, through the length of time it had abode in him, had wrought

a good habit in him, so that taking but little initiation from others he showed great zeal in this matter. He kept vigil to such an extent that he often continued the whole night without sleep; and this not once but often, to the marvel of others. He ate once a day, after sunset, sometimes once in two days, and often even in four. His food was bread and salt, his drink, water only. Of flesh and wine it is superfluous even to speak, since no such thing was found with the other earnest men. A rush mat served him to sleep upon, but for the most part he lay upon the bare ground. He would not anoint himself with oil, saying it behooved young men to be earnest in training and not to seek what would enervate the body; but they must accustom it to labour, mindful of the Apostle's words, "when I am weak, then am I strong." (2 Corinthians 12:10.) "For," said he, "the fibre of the soul is then sound when the pleasures of the body are diminished." And he had come to this truly wonderful conclusion, "that progress in virtue, and retirement from the world for the sake of it, ought not to be measured by time, but by desire and fixity of purpose." He at least gave no thought to the past, but day by day, as if he were at the beginning of his discipline, applied greater pains for advancement, often repeating to himself the saying of Paul: "Forgetting the things which are behind and stretching forward to the things which are before." (Philippians 3:14.) He was also mindful of the words spoken by the prophet Elias, "the Lord lives before whose presence I stand today." (1 Kings 18:15.) For he observed that in saying 'today' the prophet did not compute the time that had gone by: but daily as though ever commencing he eagerly endeavoured to make himself fit to appear before God, being pure in heart and ever ready to submit to His counsel, and to Him alone. And he used to say to himself that from the life of the great Elias the hermit ought to see his own as in a mirror.

His life in the tombs, and combats with demons there

8. Thus tightening his hold upon himself, Antony departed to the tombs, which happened to be at a distance from the village; and having bid one of his acquaintances to bring him bread at intervals of many days, he entered one of the tombs, and the other having shut the door on him, he remained within alone. And when the enemy could not endure it, but was even fearful that in a short time Antony would fill the desert with the discipline, coming one night with a multitude of demons, he so cut him with stripes that he lay on the ground speechless from the excessive pain. For he affirmed that the torture had been so excessive that no blows inflicted by man could ever have caused him such torment. But by the Providence of God—for the Lord never overlooks them that hope in Him—the next day his acquaintance came bringing him the loaves. And having opened the door and seeing him lying on the ground as though dead, he lifted him up and carried him to the church in the village, and laid him upon the ground. And many of his kinsfolk and the villagers sat around Antony as round a corpse. But about midnight he came to himself and arose, and when he saw them all asleep and his comrade alone watching, he motioned with his head for him to approach, and asked him to carry him again to the tombs without waking anybody.

9. He was carried therefore by the man, and as he was wont, when the door was shut he was within alone. And he could not stand up on account of the blows, but he prayed as he lay. And

after he had prayed, he said with a shout, Here am I, Antony; I flee not from your stripes, for even if you inflict more nothing shall separate me from the love of Christ. (Romans 8:35.) And then he sang, "though a camp be set against me, my heart shall not be afraid." (Psalm 27:3.) These were the thoughts and words of this ascetic. But the enemy, who hates good, marvelling that after the blows he dared to return, called together his hounds and burst forth, "You see," said he, "that neither by the spirit of lust nor by blows did we stay the man, but that he braves us, let us attack him in another fashion." But changes of form for evil are easy for the devil, so in the night they made such a din that the whole of that place seemed to be shaken by an earthquake, and the demons as if breaking the four walls of the dwelling seemed to enter through them, coming in the likeness of beasts and creeping things. And the place was on a sudden filled with the forms of lions, bears, leopards, bulls, serpents, asps, scorpions, and wolves, and each of them was moving according to his nature. The lion was roaring, wishing to attack, the bull seeming to toss with its horns, the serpent writhing but unable to approach, and the wolf as it rushed on was restrained; altogether the noises of the apparitions, with their angry ragings, were dreadful. But Antony, stricken and goaded by them, felt bodily pains severer still. He lay watching, however, with unshaken soul, groaning from bodily anguish; but his mind was clear, and as in mockery he said, "If there had been any power in you, it would have sufficed had one of you come, but since the Lord has made you weak, you attempt to terrify me by numbers: and a proof of your weakness is that you take the shapes of brute beasts." And again with boldness he said, "If you are able, and have received power against me, delay not to attack; but if you are unable, why trouble me in vain? For faith in our Lord is a seal and a wall of safety to us." So after many attempts they gnashed their teeth upon him, because they were mocking themselves rather than him.

10. Nor was the Lord then forgetful of Antony's wrestling, but was at hand to help him. So looking up he saw the roof as it were opened, and a ray of light descending to him. The demons suddenly vanished, the pain of his body straightway ceased, and the building was again whole. But Antony feeling the help, and getting his breath again, and being freed from pain, besought the vision which had appeared to him, saying, "Where were thou? Why did you not appear at the beginning to make my pains to cease?" And a voice came to him, "Antony, I was here, but I waited to see your fight; wherefore since you have endured, and hast not been worsted, I will ever be a succour to you, and will make your name known everywhere." Having heard this, Antony arose and prayed, and received such strength that he perceived that he had more power in his body than formerly. And he was then about thirty-five years old.

He goes to the desert and overcomes temptations on the way

11. And on the day following he went forth still more eagerly bent on the service of God and having fallen in with the old man he had met previously, he asked him to dwell with him in the desert. But when the other declined on account of his great age, and because as yet there was no such custom, Antony himself

set off immediately to the mountain. And yet again the enemy seeing his zeal and wishing to hinder it, cast in his way what seemed to be a great silver dish. But Antony, seeing the guile of the Evil One, stood, and having looked on the dish, he put the devil in it to shame, saying, "Whence comes a dish in the desert? This road is not well-worn, nor is there here a trace of any wayfarer; it could not have fallen without being missed on account of its size; and he who had lost it having turned back, to seek it, would have found it, for it is a desert place. This is some wile of the devil. O thou Evil One, not with this shall you hinder my purpose; let it go with you to destruction." (Acts 8:20.) And when Antony had said this it vanished like smoke from the face of fire.

How Antony took up his abode in a ruined fort across the Nile, and how he defeated the demons. His twenty years sojourn there

12. Then again as he went on he saw what was this time not visionary, but real gold scattered in the way. But whether the devil showed it, or some better power to try the athlete and show the Evil One that Antony truly cared nought for money, neither he told nor do we know. But it is certain that that which appeared was gold. And Antony marvelled at the quantity, but passed it by as though he were going over fire; so he did not even turn, but hurried on at a run to lose sight of the place. More and more confirmed in his purpose, he hurried to the mountain, and having found a fort, so long deserted that it was full of creeping things, on the other side of the river; he crossed over to it and dwelt there.

The reptiles, as though some one were chasing them, immediately left the place. But he built up the entrance completely, having stored up loaves for six months—this is a custom of the Thebans, and the loaves often remain fresh a whole year—and as he found water within, he descended as into a shrine, and abode within by himself, never going forth nor looking at any one who came. Thus he employed a long time training himself, and received loaves, let down from above, twice in the year.

13. But those of his acquaintances who came, since he did not permit them to enter, often used to spend days and nights outside, and heard as it were crowds within clamouring, dinning, sending forth piteous voices and crying, "Go from what is ours. What do you even in the desert? You can not abide our attack." So at first those outside thought there were some men fighting with him, and that they had entered by ladders; but when stooping down they saw through a hole there was nobody, they were afraid, accounting them to be demons, and they called on Antony. Them he quickly heard, though he had not given a thought to the demons, and coming to the door he besought them to depart and not to be afraid, "for thus," said he, "the demons make their seeming onslaughts against those who are cowardly. Sign yourselves therefore with the cross, and depart boldly, and let these make sport for themselves." So they departed fortified with the sign of the Cross. But he remained in no wise harmed by the evil spirits, nor was he wearied with the contest, for there came to his aid visions from above, and the weakness of the foe relieved him of much trouble and armed him with greater zeal. For his acquaintances used often to come expecting to find him dead,

and would hear him singing, "Let God arise and let His enemies be scattered, let them also that hate Him flee before His face. As smoke vanishes, let them vanish; as wax melts before the face of fire, so let the sinners perish from the face of God;" (Psalm 68:1-2.) and again, "All nations compassed me about, and in the name of the Lord I requited them." (Psalm 118:10.)

How he left the fort, and how monasticism began to flourish in Egypt. Antony its leader

14. And so for nearly twenty years he continued training himself in solitude, never going forth, and but seldom seen by any. After this, when many were eager and wishful to imitate his discipline, and his acquaintances came and began to cast down and wrench off the door by force, Antony, as from a shrine, came forth initiated in the mysteries and filled with the Spirit of God. Then for the first time he was seen outside the fort by those who came to see him. And they, when they saw him, wondered at the sight, for he had the same habit of body as before, and was neither fat, like a man without exercise, nor lean from fasting and striving with the demons, but he was just the same as they had known him before his retirement. And again his soul was free from blemish, for it was neither contracted as if by grief, nor relaxed by pleasure, nor possessed by laughter or dejection, for he was not troubled when he beheld the crowd, nor overjoyed at being saluted by so many. But he was altogether even as being guided by reason, and abiding in a natural state. Through him the Lord healed the bodily ailments of many present, and cleansed others from evil spirits. And He gave grace to Antony in speaking, so

that he consoled many that were sorrowful, and set those at variance at one, exhorting all to prefer the love of Christ before all that is in the world. And while he exhorted and advised them to remember the good things to come, and the loving-kindness of God towards us, "Who spared not His own Son, but delivered Him up for us all," (Romans 8:32) he persuaded many to embrace the solitary life. And thus it happened in the end that cells arose even in the mountains, and the desert was colonised by monks, who came forth from their own people, and enrolled themselves for the citizenship in the heavens.

15. But when he was obliged to cross the Arsenoitic Canal—and the occasion of it was the visitation of the brethren—the canal was full of crocodiles. And by simply praying, he entered it, and all they with him, and passed over in safety. And having returned to his cell, he applied himself to the same noble and valiant exercises; and by frequent conversation he increased the eagerness of those already monks, stirred up in most of the rest the love of the discipline, and speedily by the attraction of his words cells multiplied, and he directed them all as a father.

His address to monks, rendered from Coptic, exhorting them to perseverance, and encouraging them against the wiles of Satan

16. One day when he had gone forth because all the monks had assembled to him and asked to hear words from him, he spoke to them in the Egyptian tongue as follows: "The Scriptures are enough for instruction, but it is a good thing to encourage one another in the faith, and to stir up with words. Wherefore you, as

children, carry that which you know to your father; and I as the elder share my knowledge and what experience has taught me with you. Let this especially be the common aim of all, neither to give way having once begun, nor to faint in trouble, nor to say: We have lived in the discipline a long time: but rather as though making a beginning daily let us increase our earnestness. For the whole life of man is very short, measured by the ages to come, wherefore all our time is nothing compared with eternal life. And in the world everything is sold at its price, and a man exchanges one equivalent for another; but the promise of eternal life is bought for a trifle. For it is written, 'The days of our life in them are threescore years and ten, but if they are in strength, fourscore years, and what is more than these is labour and sorrow.' (Psalm 90:10.) Whenever, therefore, we live full fourscore years, or even a hundred in the discipline, not for a hundred years only shall we reign, but instead of a hundred we shall reign for ever and ever. And though we fought on earth, we shall not receive our inheritance on earth, but we have the promises in heaven; and having put off the body which is corrupt, we shall receive it incorrupt.

17. "Wherefore, children, let us not faint nor deem that the time is long, or that we are doing something great, 'for the sufferings of this present time are not worthy to be compared with the glory which shall be revealed to us-ward.' (Romans 8:18.) Nor let us think, as we look at the world, that we have renounced anything of much consequence, for the whole earth is very small compared with all the heaven. Wherefore if it even chanced that we were lords of all the earth and gave it all up, it would

be nought worthy of comparison with the kingdom of heaven. For as if a man should despise a copper drachma to gain a hundred drachmas of gold; so if a man were lord of all the earth and were to renounce it, that which he gives up is little, and he receives a hundredfold. But if not even the whole earth is equal in value to the heavens, then he who has given up a few acres leaves as it were nothing; and even if he have given up a house or much gold he ought not to boast nor be low-spirited. Further, we should consider that even if we do not relinquish them for virtue's sake, still afterwards when we die we shall leave them behind—very often, as the Preacher says, (Ecclesiastes 4:8; 6:2) to those to whom we do not wish. Why then should we not give them up for virtue's sake, that we may inherit even a kingdom? Therefore let the desire of possession take hold of no one, for what gain is it to acquire these things which we cannot take with us? Why not rather get those things which we can take away with us—to wit, prudence, justice, temperance, courage, understanding, love, kindness to the poor, faith in Christ, freedom from wrath, hospitality? If we possess these, we shall find them of themselves preparing for us a welcome there in the land of the meek-hearted.

18. "And so from such things let a man persuade himself not to make light of it, especially if he considers that he himself is the servant of the Lord, and ought to serve his Master. Wherefore as a servant would not dare to say, because I worked yesterday, I will not work today; and considering the past will do no work in the future; but, as it is written in the Gospel, daily shows the same readiness to please his master, and to avoid risk: so let us

daily abide firm in our discipline, knowing that if we are careless for a single day the Lord will not pardon us, for the sake of the past, but will be wrath against us for our neglect. As also we have heard in Ezekiel; (Ezekiel 18:26) and as Judas because of one night destroyed his previous labour.

19. "Wherefore, children, let us hold fast our discipline, and let us not be careless. For in it the Lord is our fellow-worker, as it is written, 'to all that choose the good, God works with them for good.' (Romans 8:28.) But to avoid being heedless, it is good to consider the word of the Apostle, 'I die daily.' (1 Corinthians 15:31.) For if we too live as though dying daily, we shall not sin. And the meaning of that saying is, that as we rise day by day we should think that we shall not abide till evening; and again, when about to lie down to sleep, we should think that we shall not rise up. For our life is naturally uncertain, and Providence allots it to us daily. But thus ordering our daily life, we shall neither fall into sin, nor have a lust for anything, nor cherish wrath against any, nor shall we heap up treasure upon earth. But, as though under the daily expectation of death, we shall be without wealth, and shall forgive all things to all men, nor shall we retain at all the desire of women or of any other foul pleasure. But we shall turn from it as past and gone, ever striving and looking forward to the day of Judgment. For the greater dread and danger of torment ever destroys the ease of pleasure, and sets up the soul if it is like to fall.

20. "Wherefore having already begun and set out in the way of virtue, let us strive the more that we may attain those things that are before. And let no one turn to the things behind, like Lot's

wife, all the more so that the Lord has said, 'No man, having put his hand to the plough, and turning back, is fit for the kingdom of heaven.' (Philippians 3:13; Genesis 19:26; Luke 9:62.) And this turning back is nought else but to feel regret, and to be once more worldly-minded. But fear not to hear of virtue, nor be astonished at the name. For it is not far from us, nor is it without ourselves, but it is within us, and is easy if only we are willing. That they may get knowledge, the Greeks live abroad and cross the sea, but we have no need to depart from home for the sake of the kingdom of heaven, nor to cross the sea for the sake of virtue. For the Lord aforetime has said, 'The kingdom of heaven is within you.' (Luke 17:21.) Wherefore virtue has need at our hands of willingness alone, since it is in us and is formed from us. For when the soul has its spiritual faculty in a natural state virtue is formed. And it is in a natural state when it remains as it came into existence. And when it came into existence it was fair and exceeding honest. For this cause Joshua, the son of Nun, in his exhortation said to the people, 'Make straight your heart unto the Lord God of Israel,' (Joshua 24:23) and John, 'Make your paths straight.' (Matthew 3:3.) For rectitude of soul consists in its having its spiritual part in its natural state as created. But on the other hand, when it swerves and turns away from its natural state, that is called vice of the soul. Thus the matter is not difficult. If we abide as we have been made, we are in a state of virtue, but if we think of ignoble things we shall be accounted evil. If, therefore, this thing had to be acquired from without, it would be difficult in reality; but if it is in us, let us keep ourselves from foul thoughts. And as we have received the soul as a deposit, let us preserve it for the

Lord, that He may recognise His work as being the same as He made it.

21. "And let us strive that wrath rule us not nor lust overcome us, for it is written, 'The wrath of man works not the righteousness of God. And lust, when it has conceived, bears sin, and the sin when it is full grown brings forth death.' (James 1:20, 15) Thus living, let us keep guard carefully, and as it is written, 'keep our hearts with all watchfulness'. (Proverbs 4:23.) For we have terrible and crafty foes—the evil spirits—and against them we wrestle, as the Apostle said, 'Not against flesh and blood, but against the principalities and against the powers, against the world rulers of this darkness, against the spiritual hosts of wickedness in the heavenly places.' (Ephesians 6:12.) Great is their number in the air around us, and they are not far from us. Now there are great distinctions among them; and concerning their nature and distinctions much could be said, but such a description is for others of greater powers than we possess. But at this time it is pressing and necessary for us only to know their wiles against ourselves.

22. "First, therefore, we must know this: that the demons have not been created like what we mean when we call them by that name; for God made nothing evil, but even they have been made good. Having fallen, however, from the heavenly wisdom, since then they have been grovelling on earth. On the one hand they deceived the Greeks with their displays, while out of envy of us Christians they move all things in their desire to hinder us from entry into the heavens; in order that we should not ascend up there from whence they fell. Thus there is need of much prayer and of discipline, that when a man has received through

the Spirit the gift of discerning spirits, he may have power to
recognise their characteristics: which of them are less and which
more evil; of what nature is the special pursuit of each, and how
each of them is overthrown and cast out. For their villainies and
the changes in their plots are many. The blessed Apostle and
his followers knew such things when they said, 'for we are not
ignorant of his devices;' (2 Corinthians 2:11) and we, from the
temptations we have suffered at their hands, ought to correct
one another under them. Wherefore I, having had proof of them,
speak as to children.

23. "The demons, therefore, if they see all Christians, and
monks especially, labouring cheerfully and advancing, first make
an attack by temptation and place hindrances to hamper our way,
to wit, evil thoughts. But we need not fear their suggestions, for
by prayer, fasting, and faith in the Lord their attack immediately
fails. But even when it does they cease not, but knavishly by
subtlety come on again. For when they cannot deceive the heart
openly with foul pleasures they approach in different guise, and
thenceforth shaping displays they attempt to strike fear, changing
their shapes, taking the forms of women, wild beasts, creeping
things, gigantic bodies, and troops of soldiers. But not even then
need you fear their deceitful displays. For they are nothing and
quickly disappear, especially if a man fortify himself beforehand
with faith and the sign of the cross. Yet are they bold and very
shameless, for if thus they are worsted they make an onslaught in
another manner, and pretend to prophesy and foretell the future,
and to show themselves of a height reaching to the roof and of
great breadth; that they may stealthily catch by such displays

those who could not be deceived by their arguments. If here also they find the soul strengthened by faith and a hopeful mind, then they bring their leader to their aid.

24. "And he said they often appeared as the Lord revealed the devil to Job, saying, 'His eyes are as the morning star. From his mouth proceed burning lamps and hearths of fire are cast forth. The smoke of a furnace blazing with the fire of coals proceeds from his nostrils. His breath is coals and from his mouth issues flame.' (Job 41:18-20.) When the prince of the demons appears in this wise, the crafty one, as I said before, strikes terror by speaking great things, as again the Lord convicted him saying to Job, 'for he counts iron as straw, and brass as rotten wood, yea he counts the sea as a pot of ointment, and the depth of the abyss as a captive, and the abyss as a covered walk.' (Job 41:27.) And by the prophet, 'the enemy said, I will pursue and overtake', (Exodus 15:9) and again by another, 'I will grasp the whole world in my hand as a nest, and take it up as eggs that have been left.' (Isaiah 10:14.) Such, in a word, are their boasts and professions that they may deceive the godly. But not even then ought we, the faithful, to fear his appearance or give heed to his words. For he is a liar and speaks of truth never a word. And though speaking words so many and so great in his boldness, without doubt, like a dragon he was drawn with a hook by the Saviour, (Job 41:1) and as a beast of burden he received the halter round his nostrils, and as a runaway his nostrils were bound with a ring, and his lips bored with an armlet. (Job 41:2. Cf. Job 40:19-24.) And he was bound by the Lord as a sparrow, that we should mock him. And with him are placed the demons his fellows, like serpents

and scorpions to be trodden underfoot by us Christians. And the proof of this is that we now live opposed to him. For he who threatened to dry the sea and seize upon the world, behold now cannot stay our discipline, nor even me speaking against him. Let us then heed not his words, for he is a liar: and let us not fear his visions, seeing that they themselves are deceptive. For that which appears in them is no true light, but they are rather the preludes and likenesses of the fire prepared for the demons who attempt to terrify men with those flames in which they themselves will be burned. Doubtless they appear; but in a moment disappear again, hurting none of the faithful, but bringing with them the likeness of that fire which is about to receive themselves. Wherefore it is unfitting that we should fear them on account of these things; for through the grace of Christ all their practices are in vain.

25. "Again they are treacherous, and are ready to change themselves into all forms and assume all appearances. Very often also without appearing they imitate the music of harp and voice, and recall the words of Scripture. Sometimes, too, while we are reading they immediately repeat many times, like an echo, what is read. They arouse us from our sleep to prayers; and this constantly, hardly allowing us to sleep at all. At another time they assume the appearance of monks and feign the speech of holy men, that by their similarity they may deceive and thus drag their victims where they will. But no heed must be paid them even if they arouse to prayer, even if they counsel us not to eat at all, even though they seem to accuse and cast shame upon us for those things which once they allowed. For they do this not for the sake of piety or truth, but that they may carry off the simple

to despair; and that they may say the discipline is useless, and make men loathe the solitary life as a trouble and burden, and hinder those who in spite of them walk in it.

26. "Wherefore the prophet sent by the Lord declared them to be wretched, saying: 'Woe is he who gives his neighbours to drink muddy destruction.' (Habakkuk 2:15.) For such practices and devices are subversive of the way which leads to virtue. And the Lord Himself, even if the demons spoke the truth—for they said truly 'You are the Son of God' (Luke 4:41)—still bridled their mouths and suffered them not to speak; lest haply they should sow their evil along with the truth, and that He might accustom us never to give heed to them even though they appear to speak what is true. For it is unseemly that we, having the holy Scriptures and freedom from the Saviour, should be taught by the devil who has not kept his own order but has gone from one mind to another. Wherefore even when he uses the language of Scripture He forbids him, saying: 'But to the sinner said God, Wherefore do you declare My ordinances and take My covenant in your mouth?' (Psalm 50:16.) For the demons do all things—they prate, they confuse, they dissemble, they confound—to deceive the simple. They din, laugh madly, and whistle; but if no heed is paid to them immediately they weep and lament as though vanquished.

27. "The Lord therefore, as God, stayed the mouths of the demons: and it is fitting that we, taught by the saints, should do like them and imitate their courage. For they when they saw these things used to say: 'When the sinner rose against me, I was dumb and humble, and kept silence from good words.'(Psalm

39:2.) And again: 'But I was as a deaf man and heard not, and as a dumb man who opens not his mouth, and I became as a man who hears not.' (Psalm 38:14.) So let us neither hear them as being strangers to us, nor give heed to them even though they arouse us to prayer and speak concerning fasting. But let us rather apply ourselves to our resolve of discipline, and let us not be deceived by them who do all things in deceit, even though they threaten death. For they are weak and can do nought but threaten.

28. "Already in passing I have spoken on these things, and now I must not shrink from speaking on them at greater length, for to put you in remembrance will be a source of safety. Since the Lord visited earth, the enemy is fallen and his powers weakened. Wherefore although he could do nothing, still like a tyrant, he did not bear his fall quietly, but threatened, though his threats were words only. And let each one of you consider this, and he will be able to despise the demons. Now if they were hampered with such bodies as we are, it would be possible for them to say, 'Men when they are hidden we cannot find, but whenever we do find them we do them hurt.' And we also by lying in concealment could escape them, shutting the doors against them. But if they are not of such a nature as this, but are able to enter in, though the doors be shut, and haunt all the air, both they and their leader the devil, and are wishful for evil and ready to injure; and, as the Saviour said, 'From the beginning the devil is a manslayer and a father of vice;' (John 8:44) while we, though this is so, are alive, and spend our lives all the more in opposing him; it is plain they are powerless. For place is no hindrance to their plots, nor do they look on us as friends that they should spare us; nor are

they lovers of good that they should amend. But on the contrary they are evil, and nothing is so much sought after by them as wounding them that love virtue and fear God. But since they have no power to effect anything, they do nought but threaten. But if they could, they would not hesitate, but immediately work evil (for all their desire is set on this), and especially against us. Behold now we are gathered together and speak against them, and they know when we advance they grow weak. If therefore they had power they would permit none of us Christians to live, for godliness is an abomination to a sinner. (Sirach 1:25) But since they can do nothing they inflict the greater wounds on themselves; for they can fulfil none of their threats. Next this ought to be considered, that we may be in no fear of them: that if they had the power they would not come in crowds, nor fashion displays, nor with change of form would they frame deceits. But it would suffice that one only should come and accomplish that which he was both able and willing to do: especially as every one who has the power neither slays with display nor strikes fear with tumult, but immediately makes full use of his authority as he wishes. But the demons as they have no power are like actors on the stage changing their shape and frightening children with tumultuous apparition and various forms: from which they ought rather to be despised as showing their weakness. At least the true angel of the Lord sent against the Assyrian had no need for tumults nor displays from without, nor noises nor rattlings, but in quiet he used his power and immediately destroyed a hundred and eighty-five thousand. But demons like these, who have no power, try to terrify at least by their displays. (2 Kings 19:35.)

29. "But if any one having in mind the history of Job (Job 1 and 2) should say, Why then has the devil gone forth and accomplished all things against him; and stripped him of all his possessions, and slew his children, and smote him with evil ulcers? Let such a one, on the other hand, recognise that the devil was not the strong man, but God who delivered Job to him to be tried. Certainly he had no power to do anything, but he asked, and having received it, he has wrought what he did. So also from this the enemy is the more to be condemned, for although willing he could not prevail against one just man. For if he could have, he would not have asked permission. But having asked not once but also a second time, he shows his weakness and want of power. And it is no wonder if he could do nothing against Job, when destruction would not have come even on his cattle had not God allowed it. And he has not the power over swine, for as it is written in the Gospel, they besought the Lord, saying, 'Let us enter the swine.' (Matthew 8:31.) But if they had power not even against swine, much less have they any over men formed in the image of God.

30. "So then we ought to fear God only, and despise the demons, and be in no fear of them. But the more they do these things the more let us intensify our discipline against them, for a good life and faith in God is a great weapon. At any rate they fear the fasting, the sleeplessness, the prayers, the meekness, the quietness, the contempt of money and vainglory, the humility, the love of the poor, the alms, the freedom from anger of the ascetics, and, chief of all, their piety towards Christ. Wherefore they do all things that they may not have any that trample on

them, knowing the grace given to the faithful against them by the Saviour, when He says, 'Behold I have given to you power to tread upon serpents and scorpions, and upon all the power of the enemy.' (Luke 10:19.)

31. "Wherefore if they pretend to foretell the future, let no one give heed, for often they announce beforehand that the brethren are coming days after. And they do come. The demons, however, do this not from any care for the hearers, but to gain their trust, and that then at length, having got them in their power, they may destroy them. Whence we must give no heed to them, but ought rather to confute them when speaking, since we do not need them. For what wonder is it, if with more subtle bodies than men have, when they have seen them start on their journey, they surpass them in speed, and announce their coming? Just as a horseman getting a start of a man on foot announces the arrival of the latter beforehand, so in this there is no need for us to wonder at them. For they know none of those things which are not yet in existence; but God only is He who knows all things before their birth. (Daniel 13:42.) But these, like thieves, running off first with what they see, proclaim it: to how many already have they announced our business—that we are assembled together, and discuss measures against them, before any one of us could go and tell these things. This in good truth a fleet-footed boy could do, getting far ahead of one less swift. But what I mean is this. If any one begins to walk from the Thebaid, or from any other district, before he begins to walk, they do not know whether he will walk. But when they have seen him walking they run on, and before he comes up report his approach. And so it falls out

that after a few days the travellers arrive. But often the walkers turn back, and the demons prove false.

32. "So, too, with respect to the water of the river, they sometimes make foolish statements. For having seen that there has been much rain in the regions of Ethiopia, and knowing that they are the cause of the flood of the river before the water has come to Egypt they run on and announce it. And this men could have told, if they had as great power of running as the demons. And as David's spy (2 Samuel 18:24) going up to a lofty place saw the man approaching better than one who stayed down below, and the forerunner himself announced, before the others came up, not those things which had not taken place, but those things which were already on the way and were being accomplished, so these also prefer to labour, and declare what is happening to others simply for the sake of deceiving them. If, however, Providence meantime plans anything different for the waters or wayfarers—for Providence can do this—the demons are deceived, and those who gave heed to them cheated.

33. "Thus in days gone by arose the oracles of the Greeks, and thus they were led astray by the demons. But thus also thenceforth their deception was brought to an end by the coming of the Lord, who brought to nought the demons and their devices. For they know nothing of themselves, but, like thieves, what they get to know from others they pass on, and guess at rather than foretell things. Therefore if sometimes they speak the truth, let no one marvel at them for this. For experienced physicians also, since they see the same malady in different people, often foretell what it is, making it out by their acquaintance with it. Pilots,

too, and farmers, from their familiarity with the weather, tell at a glance the state of the atmosphere, and forecast whether it will be stormy or fine. And no one would say that they do this by inspiration, but from experience and practice. So if the demons sometimes do the same by guesswork, let no one wonder at it or heed them. For what use to the hearers is it to know from them what is going to happen before the time? Or what concern have we to know such things, even if the knowledge be true? For it is not productive of virtue, nor is it any token of goodness. For none of us is judged for what he knows not, and no one is called blessed because he has learning and knowledge. But each one will be called to judgment in these points—whether he have kept the faith and truly observed the commandments.

34. "Wherefore there is no need to set much value on these things, nor for the sake of them to practise a life of discipline and labour; but that living well we may please God. And we neither ought to pray to know the future, nor to ask for it as the reward of our discipline; but our prayer should be that the Lord may be our fellow-helper for victory over the devil. And if even once we have a desire to know the future, let us be pure in mind, for I believe that if a soul is perfectly pure and in its natural state, it is able, being clear-sighted, to see more and further than the demons—for it has the Lord who reveals to it—like the soul of Elisha, which saw what was done by Gehazi, (2 Kings 5:26) and beheld the hosts standing on its side. (2 Kings 6:17.)

35. "When, therefore, they come by night to you and wish to tell the future, or say, 'we are the angels,' give no heed, for they lie. Yea even if they praise your discipline and call you

blessed, hear them not, and have no dealings with them; but rather sign yourselves and your houses, and pray, and you shall see them vanish. For they are cowards, and greatly fear the sign of the Lord's Cross, since of a truth in it the Saviour stripped them, and made an example of them. (Colossians 2:15.) But if they shamelessly stand their ground, capering and changing their forms of appearance, fear them not, nor shrink, nor heed them as though they were good spirits. For the presence either of the good or evil by the help of God can easily be distinguished. The vision of the holy ones is not fraught with distraction: 'For they will not strive, nor cry, nor shall any one hear their voice.' (Matthew 12:19; cf. Isaiah 42:2.) But it comes so quietly and gently that immediately joy, gladness and courage arise in the soul. For the Lord who is our joy is with them, and the power of God the Father. And the thoughts of the soul remain unruffled and undisturbed, so that it, enlightened as it were with rays, beholds by itself those who appear. For the love of what is divine and of the things to come possesses it, and willingly it would be wholly joined with them if it could depart along with them. But if, being men, some fear the vision of the good, those who appear immediately take fear away; as Gabriel did in the case of Zacharias, (Luke 1:13) and as the angel did who appeared to the women at the holy sepulchre, (Matthew 28:5) and as He did who said to the shepherds in the Gospel, 'Fear not.' For their fear arose not from timidity, but from the recognition of the presence of superior beings. Such then is the nature of the visions of the holy ones.

36. "But the inroad and the display of the evil spirits is fraught with confusion, with din, with sounds and cryings such as the

disturbance of boorish youths or robbers would occasion. From which arise fear in the heart, tumult and confusion of thought, dejection, hatred towards them who live a life of discipline, indifference, grief, remembrance of kinsfolk and fear of death, and finally desire of evil things, disregard of virtue and unsettled habits. Whenever, therefore, you have seen ought and are afraid, if your fear is immediately taken away and in place of it comes joy unspeakable, cheerfulness, courage, renewed strength, calmness of thought and all those I named before, boldness and love toward God—take courage and pray. For joy and a settled state of soul show the holiness of him who is present. Thus Abraham beholding the Lord rejoiced; (John 8:56) so also John at the voice of Mary, the God-bearer, leaped for gladness. (Luke 1:41.) But if at the appearance of any there is confusion, knocking without, worldly display, threats of death and the other things which I have already mentioned, know that it is an onslaught of evil spirits.

37. "And let this also be a token for you: whenever the soul remains fearful there is a presence of the enemies. For the demons do not take away the fear of their presence as the great archangel Gabriel did for Mary and Zacharias, and as he did who appeared to the women at the tomb; but rather whenever they see men afraid they increase their delusions that men may be terrified the more; and at last attacking they mock them, saying, 'fall down and worship.' Thus they deceived the Greeks, and thus by them they were considered gods, falsely so called. But the Lord did not suffer us to be deceived by the devil, for He rebuked him whenever he framed such delusions against Him, saying: 'Get

behind me, Satan: for it is written, You shall worship the Lord your God, and Him only shall you serve.' (Matthew 4:10.) More and more, therefore, let the deceiver be despised by us; for what the Lord has said, this for our sakes He has done: that the demons hearing like words from us may be put to flight through the Lord who rebuked them in those words.

38. "And it is not fitting to boast at the casting forth of the demons, nor to be uplifted by the healing of diseases: nor is it fitting that he who casts out devils should alone be highly esteemed, while he who casts them not out should be considered nought. But let a man learn the discipline of each one and either imitate, rival, or correct it. For the working of signs is not ours but the Saviour's work: and so He said to His disciples: 'Rejoice not that the demons are subject to you, but that your names are written in the heavens.' (Luke 10:20.) For the fact that our names are written in heaven is a proof of our virtuous life, but to cast out demons is a favour of the Saviour who granted it. Wherefore to those who boasted in signs but not in virtue, and said: 'Lord, in Your name did we not cast out demons, and in Your name did many mighty works?' (Matthew 7:22.) He answered, 'Verily I say unto you, I know you not;' for the Lord knows not the ways of the wicked. But we ought always to pray, as I said above, that we may receive the gift of discerning spirits; that, as it is written, (1 John 4:1) we may not believe every spirit.

39. "I should have liked to speak no further and to say nothing from my own promptings, satisfied with what I have said: but lest you should think that I speak at random and believe that I detail these things without experience or truth; for this cause

even though I should become as a fool, yet the Lord who hears knows the clearness of my conscience, and that it is not for my own sake, but on account of your affection towards me and at your petition that I again tell what I saw of the practices of evil spirits. How often have they called me blessed and I have cursed them in the name of the Lord! How often have they predicted the rising of the river, and I answered them, 'What have you to do with it?' Once they came threatening and surrounded me like soldiers in full armour. At another time they filled the house with horses, wild beasts and creeping things, and I sang: 'Some in chariots and some in horses, but we will boast in the name of the Lord our God;' (Psalm 20:7.) and at the prayers they were turned to flight by the Lord. Once they came in darkness, bearing the appearance of a light, and said, 'We have come to give you a light, Antony.' But I closed my eyes and prayed, and immediately the light of the wicked ones was quenched. And a few months after they came as though singing psalms and babbling the words of Scripture, 'But I like a deaf man, heard not.' (Psalm 38:14.) Once they shook the cell with an earthquake, but I continued praying with unshaken heart. And after this they came again making noises, whistling and dancing. But as I prayed and lay singing psalms to myself they immediately began to lament and weep, as if their strength had failed them. But I gave glory to the Lord who had brought down and made an example of their daring and madness.

40. "Once a demon exceeding high appeared with pomp, and dared to say, 'I am the power of God and I am Providence, what do you wish that I shall give you?' But I then so much the more

breathed upon him, and spoke the name of Christ, and set about
to smite him. And I seemed to have smitten him, and immediately
he, big as he was, together with all his demons, disappeared at
the name of Christ. At another time, while I was fasting, he came
full of craft, under the semblance of a monk, with what seemed
to be loaves, and gave me counsel, saying, 'Eat and cease from
your many labours. Thou also art a man and art like to fall sick.'
But I, perceiving his device, rose up to pray; and he endured it
not, for he departed, and through the door there seemed to go
out as it were smoke. How often in the desert has he displayed
what resembled gold, that I should only touch it and look on
it. But I sang psalms against him, and he vanished away. Often
they would beat me with stripes, and I repeated again and again,
'Nothing shall separate me from the love of Christ,' (Romans
8:35) and at this they rather fell to beating one another. Nor was
it I that stayed them and destroyed their power, but it was the
Lord, who said, 'I beheld Satan as lightning fall from Heaven;'
(Luke 10:18) but I, children, mindful of the Apostle's words, (1
Corinthians 4:6) transferred this to myself, that you might learn
not to faint in discipline, nor to fear the devil nor the delusions
of the demons.

41. "And since I have become a fool in detailing these things,
receive this also as an aid to your safety and fearlessness; and
believe me for I do not lie. Once some one knocked at the door
of my cell, and going forth I saw one who seemed of great size
and tall. Then when I enquired, 'Who are you?' he said, 'I am
Satan.' Then when I said, 'Why are you here?' he answered, 'Why
do the monks and all other Christians blame me undeservedly?

Why do they curse me hourly?' Then I answered, 'Wherefore do you trouble them?' He said, 'I am not he who troubles them, but they trouble themselves, for I have become weak. Have they not read: "The swords of the enemy have come to an end, and you have destroyed the cities?" (Psalm 9:6.) I have no longer a place, a weapon, a city. The Christians are spread everywhere, and at length even the desert is filled with monks. Let them take heed to themselves, and let them not curse me undeservedly.' Then I marvelled at the grace of the Lord, and said to him: 'You who art ever a liar and never speakest the truth, this at length, even against your will, you have truly spoken. For the coming of Christ has made you weak, and He has cast you down and stripped you.' But he having heard the Saviour's name, and not being able to bear the burning from it, vanished.

42. "If, therefore, the devil himself confesses that his power is gone, we ought utterly to despise both him and his demons; and since the enemy with his hounds has but devices of this sort, we, having got to know their weakness, are able to despise them. Wherefore let us not despond after this fashion, nor let us have a thought of cowardice in our heart, nor frame fears for ourselves, saying, I am afraid lest a demon should come and overthrow me; lest he should lift me up and cast me down; or lest rising against me on a sudden he confound me. Such thoughts let us not have in mind at all, nor let us be sorrowful as though we were perishing; but rather let us be courageous and rejoice always, believing that we are safe. Let us consider in our soul that the Lord is with us, who put the evil spirits to flight and broke their power. Let us consider and lay to heart that while the

Lord is with us, our foes can do us no hurt. For when they come they approach us in a form corresponding to the state in which they discover us, and adapt their delusions to the condition of mind in which they find us. If, therefore, they find us timid and confused, they immediately beset the place, like robbers, having found it unguarded; and what we of ourselves are thinking, they do, and more also. For if they find us faint-hearted and cowardly, they mightily increase our terror, by their delusions and threats; and with these the unhappy soul is thenceforth tormented. But if they see us rejoicing in the Lord, contemplating the bliss of the future, mindful of the Lord, deeming all things in His hand, and that no evil spirit has any strength against the Christian, nor any power at all over any one—when they behold the soul fortified with these thoughts—they are discomfited and turned backwards. Thus the enemy, seeing Job fenced round with them, withdrew from him; but finding Judas unguarded, him he took captive. Thus if we are wishful to despise the enemy, let us ever ponder over the things of the Lord, and let the soul ever rejoice in hope. And we shall see the snares of the demon are like smoke, and the evil ones themselves flee rather than pursue. For they are, as I said before, exceeding fearful, ever looking forward to the fire prepared for them.

43. "And for your fearlessness against them hold this sure sign—whenever there is any apparition, be not prostrate with fear, but whatsoever it be, first boldly ask, Who are you? And from whence do you come? And if it should be a vision of holy ones they will assure you, and change your fear into joy. But if the vision should be from the devil, immediately it becomes

feeble, beholding your firm purpose of mind. For merely to ask,
Who are you? (Joshua 5:13) And whence do you come? Is a proof
of coolness. By thus asking, the son of Nun learned who his
helper was; nor did the enemy escape the questioning of Daniel."
(Daniel 13:51-59.)

The growth of the monastic life at this time (about A.D. 305)

44. While Antony was thus speaking all rejoiced; in some the
love of virtue increased, in others carelessness was thrown aside,
the self-conceit of others was stopped; and all were persuaded to
despise the assaults of the Evil One, and marvelled at the grace
given to Antony from the Lord for the discerning of spirits. So
their cells were in the mountains, like filled with holy bands of
men who sang psalms, loved reading, fasted, prayed, rejoiced in
the hope of things to come, laboured in almsgiving, and preserved
love and harmony one with another. And truly it was possible,
as it were, to behold a land set by itself, filled with piety and
justice. For then there was neither the evil-doer, nor the injured,
nor the reproaches of the tax-gatherer: but instead a multitude
of ascetics; and the one purpose of them all was to aim at virtue.
So that any one beholding the cells again, and seeing such good
order among the monks, would lift up his voice and say, "How
goodly are your dwellings, O Jacob, and your tents, O Israel; as
shady glens and as a garden by a river; as tents which the Lord
has pitched, and like cedars near waters." (Numbers 24:5-6.)

How Antony renewed his ascetic endeavours at this time

45. Antony, however, according to his custom, returned alone to his own cell, increased his discipline, and sighed daily as he thought of the mansions in Heaven, having his desire fixed on them, and pondering over the shortness of man's life. And he used to eat and sleep, and go about all other bodily necessities with shame when he thought of the spiritual faculties of the soul. So often, when about to eat with any other hermits, recollecting the spiritual food, he begged to be excused, and departed far off from them, deeming it a matter for shame if he should be seen eating by others. He used, however, when by himself, to eat through bodily necessity, but often also with the brethren; covered with shame on these occasions, yet speaking boldly words of help. And he used to say that it behooved a man to give all his time to his soul rather than his body, yet to grant a short space to the body through its necessities; but all the more earnestly to give up the whole remainder to the soul and seek its profit, that it might not be dragged down by the pleasures of the body, but, on the contrary, the body might be in subjection to the soul. For this is that which was spoken by the Saviour: "Be not anxious for your life what you shall eat, nor for your body what you shall put on. And do you seek not what you shall eat, or what you shall drink, and be not of a doubtful mind. For all these things the nations of the world seek after. But your Father knows that you have need of all these things. Howbeit do you seek first His Kingdom, and all these things shall be added unto you" (Matthew 6:31; Luke 12:29.)

How he sought martyrdom at Alexandria during the Persecution (311)

46. After this the Church was seized by the persecution which then took place under Maximinus, and when the holy martyrs were led to Alexandria, Antony also followed, leaving his cell, and saying, Let us go too, that if called, we may contend or behold them that are contending. And he longed to suffer martyrdom, but not being willing to give himself up, he ministered to the confessors in the mines and in the prisons. And he was very zealous in the judgment hall to stir up to readiness those who were summoned when in their contest, while those who were being martyred he received and brought on their way until they were perfected. The judge, therefore, beholding the fearlessness of Antony and his companions, and their zeal in this matter, commanded that no monk should appear in the judgment hall, nor remain at all in the city. So all the rest thought it good to hide themselves that day, but Antony gave so little heed to the command that he washed his garment, and stood all next day on a raised place before them, and appeared in his best before the governor. Therefore when all the rest wondered at this, and the governor saw and passed by with his array, he stood fearlessly, showing the readiness of us Christians. For, as I said before, he prayed himself to be a martyr, wherefore he seemed as one grieved that he had not borne his witness. But the Lord was keeping him for our profit and that of others, that he should become a teacher to many of the discipline which he had learned from the Scriptures. For many only beholding his manner of life were eager to be imitators of his ways. So he again ministered

as usual to the confessors, and as though he were their fellow captive he laboured in his ministry.

How he lived at this time

47. And when at last the persecution ceased, and the blessed Bishop Peter had borne his testimony, Antony departed, and again withdrew to his cell, and was there daily a martyr to his conscience, and contending in the conflicts of faith. And his discipline was much severer, for he was ever fasting, and he had a garment of hair on the inside, while the outside was skin, which he kept until his end. And he neither bathed his body with water to free himself from filth, nor did he ever wash his feet, nor even endure so much as to put them into water, unless compelled by necessity. Nor did any one even see him unclothed, nor his body naked at all, except after his death, when he was buried.

How he delivered a woman from an evil spirit

48. When therefore he had retired and determined to fix a time, after which neither to go forth himself nor admit anybody, Martinian, a military officer, came and disturbed Antony. For he had a daughter afflicted with an evil spirit. But when he continued for a long while knocking at the door, and asking him to come out and pray to God for his child, Antony, not bearing to open, looked out from above and said, "Man, why do you call on me? I also am a man even as you. But if you believe in Christ whom I serve, go, and according as you believe, pray to God, and it shall come to pass." Straightway, therefore, he departed, believing and calling upon Christ, and he received his daughter cleansed from the devil. Many other things also through Antony the Lord did, who says,

"Seek and it shall be given unto you." (Luke 11:9.) For many of the sufferers, when he would not open his door, slept outside his cell, and by their faith and sincere prayers were healed.

How at this time he betook himself to his 'inner mountain.'

49. But when he saw himself beset by many, and not suffered to withdraw himself according to his intent as he wished, fearing because of the signs which the Lord wrought by him, that either he should be puffed up, or that some other should think of him above what he ought to think, he considered and set off to go into the upper Thebaid, among those to whom he was unknown. And having received loaves from the brethren, he sat down by the bank of the river, looking whether a boat would go by, that, having embarked thereon, he might go up the river with them. While he was considering these things, a voice came to him from above, "Antony, where are you going and why?" But he no way disturbed, but as he had been accustomed to be called often thus, giving ear to it, answered, saying, "Since the multitude permit me not to be still, I wish to go into the upper Thebaid on account of the many hindrances that come upon me here, and especially because they demand of me things beyond my power." But the voice said to him, "Even though you should go into the Thebaid, or even though, as you have in mind, you should go down to the Bucolia, you will have to endure more, aye, double the amount of toil. But if you wish really to be in quiet, depart now into the inner desert." And when Antony said, "Who will show me the way for I know it not?" immediately the voice pointed out to him

Saracens about to go that way. So Antony approached, and drew near them, and asked that he might go with them into the desert. And they, as though they had been commanded by Providence, received him willingly. And having journeyed with them three days and three nights, he came to a very lofty mountain, and at the foot of the mountain ran a clear spring, whose waters were sweet and very cold; outside there was a plain and a few uncared-for palm trees.

50. Antony then, as it were, moved by God, loved the place, for this was the spot which he who had spoken with him by the banks of the river had pointed out. So having first received loaves from his fellow travellers, he abode in the mountain alone, no one else being with him. And recognising it as his own home, he remained in that place for the future. But the Saracens, having seen the earnestness of Antony, purposely used to journey that way, and joyfully brought him loaves, while now and then the palm trees also afforded him a poor and frugal relish. But after this, the brethren learning of the place, like children mindful of their father, took care to send to him. But when Antony saw that the bread was the cause of trouble and hardships to some of them, to spare the monks this, he resolved to ask some of those who came to bring him a spade, an axe, and a little grain. And when these were brought, he went over the land round the mountain, and having found a small plot of suitable ground, tilled it; and having a plentiful supply of water for watering, he sowed. This doing year by year, he got his bread from thence, rejoicing that thus he would be troublesome to no one, and because he kept himself from being a burden to anybody. But after this, seeing

again that people came, he cultivated a few pot-herbs, that he who came to him might have some slight solace after the labour of that hard journey. At first, however, the wild beasts in the desert, coming because of the water, often injured his seeds and husbandry. But he, gently laying hold of one of them, said to them all, "Why do you hurt me, when I hurt none of you? Depart, and in the name of the Lord come not near this spot." And from that time forward, as though fearful of his command, they no more came near the place.

How he there combated the demons

51. So he was alone in the inner mountain, spending his time in prayer and discipline. And the brethren who served him asked that they might come every month and bring him olives, pulse and oil, for by now he was an old man. There then he passed his life, and endured such great wrestlings, "Not against flesh and blood," (Ephesians 6:12) as it is written, but against opposing demons, as we learned from those who visited him. For there they heard tumults, many voices, and, as it were, the clash of arms. At night they saw the mountain become full of wild beasts, and him also fighting as though against visible beings, and praying against them. And those who came to him he encouraged, while kneeling he contended and prayed to the Lord. Surely it was a marvellous thing that a man, alone in such a desert, feared neither the demons who rose up against him, nor the fierceness of the four-footed beasts and creeping things, for all they were so many. But in truth, as it is written, "He trusted in the Lord as Mount Sion," (Psalm 125:1) with a mind unshaken and undisturbed; so that the demons rather fled from him, and the wild beasts, as it is

written, "kept peace with him." (Job 5:23.)

52. The devil, therefore, as David says in the Psalms, (Psalm 35:16) observed Antony and gnashed his teeth against him. But Antony was consoled by the Saviour and continued unhurt by his wiles and varied devices. As he was watching in the night the devil sent wild beasts against him. And almost all the hyenas in that desert came forth from their dens and surrounded him; and he was in the midst, while each one threatened to bite. Seeing that it was a trick of the enemy he said to them all: "If you have received power against me I am ready to be devoured by you; but if you were sent against me by demons, stay not, but depart, for I am a servant of Christ." When Antony said this they fled, driven by that word as with a whip.

53. A few days after, as he was working (for he was careful to work hard), some one stood at the door and pulled the plait which he was working, for he used to weave baskets, which he gave to those who came in return for what they brought him. And rising up he saw a beast like a man to the thighs but having legs and feet like those of an ass. And Antony only signed himself and said, "I am a servant of Christ. If you are sent against me, behold I am here." But the beast together with his evil spirits fled, so that, through his speed, he fell and died. And the death of the beast was the fall of the demons. For they strove in all manner of ways to lead Antony from the desert and were not able.

Of the miraculous spring, and how he edified the monks of the 'outer' mountain, and of Antony's sister

54. And once being asked by the monks to come down and visit them and their abodes after a time, he journeyed with those who came to him. And a camel carried the loaves and the water for them. For all that desert is dry, and there is no water at all that is fit to drink, save in that mountain from whence they drew the water, and in which Antony's cell was. So when the water failed them on their way, and the heat was very great, they all were in danger. For having gone round the neighbourhood and finding no water, they could walk no further, but lay on the ground and despairing of themselves, let the camel go. But the old man seeing that they were all in jeopardy, groaning in deep grief, departed a little way from them, and kneeling down he stretched forth his hands and prayed. And immediately the Lord made water to well forth where he had stood praying, and so all drank and were revived. And having filled their bottles they sought the camel and found her, for the rope happened to have caught in a stone and so was held fast. Having led it and watered it they placed the bottles on its back and finished their journey in safety. And when he came to the outer cells all saluted him, looking on him as a father. And he too, as though bringing supplies from the mountain, entertained them with his words and gave them a share of help. And again there was joy in the mountains, zeal for improvement and consolation through their mutual faith. Antony also rejoiced when he beheld the earnestness of the monks, and his sister grown old in virginity, and that she herself also was the leader of other virgins.

How humanely he counselled those who resorted to him

55. So after certain days he went in again to the mountain. And henceforth many resorted to him, and others who were suffering ventured to go in. To all the monks therefore who came to him, he continually gave this precept: "Believe in the Lord and love Him; keep yourselves from filthy thoughts and fleshly pleasures, and as it is written in the Proverbs, 'be not deceived by the fullness of the belly.' (Proverbs 24:15.) Pray continually; avoid vainglory; sing psalms before sleep and on awaking; hold in your heart the commandments of Scripture; be mindful of the works of the saints that your souls being put in remembrance of the commandments may be brought into harmony with the zeal of the saints." And especially he counselled them to meditate continually on the apostle's word, "Let not the sun go down upon your wrath." (Ephesians 4:26.) And he considered this was spoken of all commandments in common, and that not on wrath alone, but not on any other sin of ours, ought the sun to go down. For it was good and needful that neither the sun should condemn us for an evil by day nor the moon for a sin by night, or even for an evil thought. That this state may be preserved in us it is good to hear the apostle and keep his words, for he says, "Try your own selves and prove your own selves." (2 Corinthians 13:5.) Daily, therefore, let each one take from himself the tale of his actions both by day and night; and if he have sinned, let him cease from it; while if he have not, let him not be boastful. But let him abide in that which is good, without being negligent, nor condemning his neighbours, nor justifying himself, "until the Lord come who searches out hidden things," (1 Corinthians 4:5; Romans 2:16) as

says the blessed apostle Paul. For often unawares we do things that we know not of; but the Lord sees all things. Wherefore committing the judgment to Him, let us have sympathy one with another. Let us bear each other's burdens: (Galatians 6:6) but let us examine our own selves and hasten to fill up that in which we are lacking. And as a safeguard against sin let the following be observed. Let us each one note and write down our actions and the impulses of our soul as though we were going to relate them to each other. And be assured that if we should be utterly ashamed to have them known, we shall abstain from sin and harbour no base thoughts in our mind. For who wishes to be seen while sinning? Or who will not rather lie after the commission of a sin, through the wish to escape notice? As then while we are looking at one another, we would not commit carnal sin, so if we record our thoughts as though about to tell them to one another, we shall the more easily keep ourselves free from vile thoughts through shame lest they should be known. Wherefore let that which is written be to us in place of the eyes of our fellow hermits, that blushing as much to write as if we had been caught, we may never think of what is unseemly. Thus fashioning ourselves we shall be able to keep the body in subjection, to please the Lord, and to trample on the devices of the enemy.

56. This was the advice he gave to those who came to him. And with those who suffered he sympathised and prayed. And oft-times the Lord heard him on behalf of many: yet he boasted not because he was heard, nor did he murmur if he were not. But always he gave the Lord thanks and besought the sufferer to be patient, and to know that healing belonged neither to him nor

to man at all, but only to the Lord, who does good when and to whom He will. The sufferers therefore used to receive the words of the old man as though they were a cure, learning not to be downhearted but rather to be long-suffering. And those who were healed were taught not to give thanks to Antony but to God alone.

Of the case of Fronto, healed by faith and prayer

57. Wherefore a man, Fronto by name, who was an officer of the Court and had a terrible disease, for he used to bite his own tongue and was in danger of injury to his eyes, having come to the mountain, asked Antony to pray for him. But Antony said to him, "Depart and you shall be healed." But when he was violent and remained within some days, Antony waited and said, "If you stay here, you can not be healed. Go, and having come into Egypt you shall see the sign wrought in you." And he believed and went. And as soon as he set eyes on Egypt his sufferings ceased, and the man became whole according to the word of Antony, which the Saviour had revealed to him in prayer.

Of a certain virgin, and of Paphnutius the confessor

58. There was also a maiden from Busiris Tripolitana, who had a terrible and very hideous disorder. For the runnings of her eyes, nose, and ears fell to the ground and immediately became worms. She was paralysed also and squinted. Her parents having heard of monks going to Antony, and believing on the Lord who healed the woman with the issue of blood, (Matthew 9:20) asked to be allowed, together with their daughter, to journey with them. And when they suffered them, the parents together with the girl,

remained outside the mountain with Paphnutius, the confessor and monk; but the monks went in to Antony. And when they only wished to tell about the damsel, he anticipated them, and detailed both the sufferings of the child and how she journeyed with them. Then when they asked that she should be admitted, Antony did not allow it, but said, "Go, and if she be not dead, you will find her healed: for the accomplishment of this is not mine, that she should come to me, wretched man that I am, but her healing is the work of the Saviour, who in every place shows His pity to them that call upon Him. Wherefore the Lord has inclined to her as she prayed, and His loving-kindness has declared to me that He will heal the child where she now is." So the wonder took place; and going out they found the parents rejoicing and the girl whole.

Of the two brethren, and how one perished of thirst

59. But when two brethren were coming to him, the water failed on the way, and one died and the other was at the point of death, for he had no strength to go on, but lay upon the ground expecting to die. But Antony sitting in the mountain called two monks, who chanced to be there, and urged them saying, "Take a pitcher of water and run on the road towards Egypt. For of two men who were coming, one is already dead and the other will die unless you hasten. For this has been revealed to me as I was praying." The monks therefore went, and found one lying dead, whom they buried, and the other they restored with water and led him to the old man. For it was a day's journey. But if any one asks, why he did not speak before the other died, the question ought not to be asked. For the punishment of death was not Antony's but

God's, who also judged the one and revealed the condition of the other. But the marvel here was only in the case of Antony: that he sitting in the mountain had his heart watchful, and had the Lord to show him things afar off.

Of the death of Amun, and Antony's vision thereof

60. And this is so, for once again he was sitting on the mountain, and looking up saw in the air some one being borne upwards, and there was much joy among those who met him. Then wondering and deeming a company of that kind to be blessed, he prayed to learn what this might be. And immediately a voice came to him: "This is the soul of Amun, the monk at Nitria." Now Amun had persevered in the discipline up to old age; and the distance from Nitria to the mountain where Antony was, was thirteen days' journey. The companions of Antony therefore, seeing the old man amazed, asked to learn, and heard that Amun was just dead. And he was well known, for he had stayed there very often, and many signs had been wrought by his means. And this is one of them. Once when he had need to cross the river called Lycus (now it was the season of the flood), he asked his comrade Theodorus to remain at a distance, that they should not see one another naked as they swam the water. Then when Theodorus was departed he again felt ashamed even to see himself naked. While, therefore, he was pondering filled with shame, on a sudden he was borne over to the other side. Theodorus, therefore, himself being a good man, approached, and seeing Amun across first without a drop of water falling from him, enquired how he had got over. And when he saw that Amun was unwilling to tell him, he held him by the feet and declared that he would not let him go before he

THE LIFE OF ST. ANTHONY, n. 59-61

had learned it from him. So Amun seeing the determination of Theodorus especially from what he had said, and having asked him to tell no man before his death, told him that he had been carried and placed on the further side. And that he had not even set foot on the water, nor was that possible for man, but for the Lord alone and those whom He permits, as He did for the great apostle Peter. (Matthew 14:28.) Theodorus therefore told this after the death of Amun. And the monks to whom Antony spoke concerning Amun's death marked the day; and when the brethren came up from Nitria thirty days after, they enquired of them and learned that Amun had fallen asleep at that day and hour in which the old man had seen his soul borne upwards. And both these and the others marvelled at the purity of Antony's soul, how he had immediately learned that which was taking place at a distance of thirteen days' journey, and had seen the soul as it was taken up.

Of Count Archelaus and the virgin Polycration

61. And Archelaus too, the Count, on a time having found him in the outer mountain, asked him merely to pray for Polycratia of Laodicea, an excellent and Christian maiden, for she suffered terribly in the stomach and side through over much discipline, and was altogether weakly of body. Antony prayed therefore, and the Count noted the day in which the prayer was made, and having departed to Laodicea he found the maiden whole. And having enquired when and on what day she was relieved of her infirmity, he produced the paper on which he had written the time of the prayer, and having read it he immediately showed the writing on the paper. And all wondered when they knew that

the Lord had relieved her of pain at the time when Antony was praying and invoking the goodness of the Saviour on her behalf.

62. And concerning those who came to him, he often foretold some days or sometimes a month beforehand what was the cause of their coming. For some came only for the sake of seeing him, others through sickness, and others suffering from evil spirits. And all thought the labour of the journey neither trouble nor loss. For each one returned aware that he had received benefit. But though saying such things and beholding such sights, he used to ask that no one should wonder at him for this; but should rather marvel at the Lord for having granted to us men to know Him as far as our powers extended.

Strange tales of the casting out of demons

63. Afterwards, on another occasion, having descended to the outer cells, he was asked to enter a vessel and pray with the monks, and he alone perceived an exceedingly unpleasant smell. But those on board said that the stench arose from the fish and salt meat in the ship. He replied however, the smell was different from that; and while he was speaking, a youth with an evil spirit, who had come and hidden himself in the ship, cried out. But the demon being rebuked in the name of the Lord Jesus Christ departed from him, and the man became whole. And all knew that the evil smell arose from the demon.

64. And another, a person of rank, came to him, possessed by a demon; and the demon was so terrible that the man possessed did not know that he was coming to Antony. But he even ate the excreta from his body. So those who brought him besought Antony to pray for him. And Antony pitying the young man

prayed and kept watch with him all the night. And about dawn the young man suddenly attacked Antony and gave him a push. But when those who came with him were angry, Antony said, "Be not angry with the young man, for it is not he, but the demon which is in him. And being rebuked and commanded to go into dry places, the demon became raging mad, and he has done this. Wherefore give thanks to the Lord, for his attack on me thus is a sign of the departure of the evil spirit." When Antony had said this, straightway the young man had become whole, and having come at last to his right mind, knew where he was, and saluted the old man and gave thanks to God.

Of Antony's vision concerning the forgiveness of his sins

65. And many monks have related with the greatest agreement and unanimity that many other such like things were done by him. But still these do not seem as marvellous as certain other things appear to be. For once, when about to eat, having risen up to pray about the ninth hour, he perceived that he was caught up in the spirit, and, wonderful to tell, he stood and saw himself, as it were, from outside himself, and that he was led in the air by certain ones. Next certain bitter and terrible beings stood in the air and wished to hinder him from passing through. But when his conductors opposed them, they demanded whether he was not accountable to them. And when they wished to sum up the account from his birth, Antony's conductors stopped them, saying, "The Lord has wiped out the sins from his birth, but from the time he became a monk, and devoted himself to God, it is

permitted you to make a reckoning." Then when they accused him and could not convict him, his way was free and unhindered. And immediately he saw himself, as it were, coming and standing by himself, and again he was Antony as before. Then forgetful of eating, he remained the rest of the day and through the whole of the night groaning and praying. For he was astonished when he saw against what mighty opponents our wrestling is, and by what labours we have to pass through the air. And he remembered that this is what the Apostle said, "according to the prince of the power of the air." (Ephesians 2:2.) For in it the enemy has power to fight and to attempt to hinder those who pass through. Wherefore most earnestly he exhorted, "Take up the whole armour of God, that you may be able to withstand in the evil day," (Ephesians 6:13) that the enemy, "having no evil thing to say against us, may be ashamed." (Titus 2:8.) And we who have learned this, let us be mindful of the Apostle when he says, "whether in the body I know not, or whether out of the body I know not; God knows." (2 Corinthians 12:2.) But Paul was caught up unto the third heaven, and having heard things unspeakable he came down; while Antony saw that he had come to the air, and contended until he was free.

Of the passage of souls, and how some were hindered of Satan

66. And he had also this favour granted him. For as he was sitting alone on the mountain, if ever he was in perplexity in his meditations, this was revealed to him by Providence in prayer. And the happy man, as it is written, was taught of God. (Isaiah

54:13; John 6:45.) After this, when he once had a discussion with certain men who had come to him concerning the state of the soul and of what nature its place will be after this life, the following night one from above called him, saying, "Antony, rise, go out and look." Having gone out therefore (for he knew whom he ought to obey) looking up, he beheld one standing and reaching to the clouds, tall, hideous, and fearful, and others ascending as though they were winged. And the figure stretched forth his hands, and some of those who were ascending were stayed by him, while others flew above, and having escaped heaven-ward, were borne aloft free from care. At such, therefore, the giant gnashed his teeth, but rejoiced over those who fell back. And immediately a voice came to Antony, "Do you understand what you see?" And his understanding was opened, and he understood that it was the passing of souls, and that the tall being who stood was the enemy who envies the faithful. And those whom he caught and stopped from passing through are accountable to him, while those whom he was unable to hold as they passed upwards had not been subservient to him. So having seen this, and as it were being reminded, he struggled the more daily to advance towards those things which were before. And these visions he was unwilling to tell, but as he spent much time in prayer, and was amazed, when those who were with him pressed him with questions and forced him, he was compelled to speak, as a father who cannot withhold ought from his children. And he thought that as his conscience was clear, the account would be beneficial for them, that they might learn that discipline bore good fruit, and that visions were oftentimes the solace of their labours.

How Antony reverenced all ordained persons

67. Added to this he was tolerant in disposition and humble in spirit. For though he was such a man, he observed the rule of the Church most rigidly, and was willing that all the clergy should be honoured above himself. For he was not ashamed to bow his head to bishops and presbyters, and if ever a deacon came to him for help he discoursed with him on what was profitable, but gave place to him in prayer, not being ashamed to learn himself. For often he would ask questions, and desired to listen to those who were present, and if any one said anything that was useful he confessed that he was profited. And besides, his countenance had a great and wonderful grace. This gift also he had from the Saviour. For if he were present in a great company of monks, and any one who did not know him previously, wished to see him, immediately coming forward he passed by the rest, and hurried to Antony, as though attracted by his appearance. Yet neither in height nor breadth was he conspicuous above others, but in the serenity of his manner and the purity of his soul. For as his soul was free from disturbances, his outward appearance was calm; so from the joy of his soul he possessed a cheerful countenance, and from his bodily movements could be perceived the condition of his soul, as it is written, "When the heart is merry the countenance is cheerful, but when it is sorrowful it is cast down." (Proverbs 15:13.) Thus Jacob recognised the counsel Laban had in his heart, and said to his wives, "The countenance of your father is not as it was yesterday and the day before." (Genesis 31:5; 1 Samuel 16:12; 17:32.) Thus Samuel recognised David, for he had mirthful eyes, and teeth white as milk. Thus

Antony was recognised, for he was never disturbed, for his soul was at peace; he was never downcast, for his mind was joyous.

How he rejected the schism of Meletius and the heresies of Manes and Arius

68. And he was altogether wonderful in faith and religious, for he never held communion with the Meletian schismatics, knowing their wickedness and apostacy from the beginning; nor had he friendly dealings with the Manichæans or any other heretics; or, if he had, only as far as advice that they should change to piety. For he thought and asserted that intercourse with these was harmful and destructive to the soul. In the same manner also he loathed the heresy of the Arians, and exhorted all neither to approach them nor to hold their erroneous belief. And once when certain Arian madmen came to him, when he had questioned them and learned their impiety, he drove them from the mountain, saying that their words were worse than the poison of serpents.

How he confuted the Arians

69. And once also the Arians having lyingly asserted that Antony's opinions were the same as theirs, he was displeased and angry against them. Then being summoned by the bishops and all the brethren, he descended from the mountain, and having entered Alexandria, he denounced the Arians, saying that their heresy was the last of all and a forerunner of Antichrist. And he taught the people that the Son of God was not a created being, neither had He come into being from non-existence, but that He was the Eternal Word and Wisdom of the Essence of the Father. And therefore it was impious to say, "there was a time when He was

not," for the Word was always co-existent with the Father. Wherefore have no fellowship with the most impious Arians. For there is no communion between light and darkness. (2 Corinthians 6:14.) For you are good Christians, but they, when they say that the Son of the Father, the Word of God, is a created being, differ in nought from the heathen, since they worship that which is created, rather than God the creator. But believe that the Creation itself is angry with them because they number the Creator, the Lord of all, by whom all things came into being, with those things which were originated.

How he visited Alexandria, and healed and converted many, and how Athanasius escorted him from the city

70. All the people, therefore, rejoiced when they heard the anti-Christian heresy anathematised by such a man. And all the people in the city ran together to see Antony; and the Greeks and those who are called their Priests, came into the church, saying, "We ask to see the man of God," for so they all called him. For in that place also the Lord cleansed many of demons, and healed those who were mad. And many Greeks asked that they might even but touch the old man, believing that they should be profited. Assuredly as many became Christians in those few days as one would have seen made in a year. Then when some thought that he was troubled by the crowds, and on this account turned them all away from him, he said, undisturbedly, that there were not more of them than of the demons with whom he wrestled in the mountain.

71. But when he was departing, and we were setting him

forth on his way, as we arrived at the gate a woman from behind cried out, "Stay, thou man of God, my daughter is grievously vexed by a devil. Stay, I beseech you, lest I too harm myself with running." And the old man when he heard her, and was asked by us, willingly stayed. And when the woman drew near, the child was cast on the ground. But when Antony had prayed and called upon the name of Christ, the child was raised whole, for the unclean spirit had gone forth. And the mother blessed God, and all gave thanks. And Antony himself also rejoiced, departing to the mountain as though it were to his own home.

How he reasoned with divers Greeks and philosophers at the 'outer' mountain

72. And Antony also was exceeding prudent, and the wonder was that although he had not learned letters, he was a ready-witted and sagacious man. At all events two Greek philosophers once came, thinking they could try their skill on Antony; and he was in the outer mountain, and having recognised who they were from their appearance, he came to them and said to them by means of an interpreter, "Why, philosophers, did ye trouble yourselves so much to come to a foolish man?" And when they said that he was not a foolish man, but exceedingly prudent, he said to them, "If you came to a foolish man, your labour is superfluous; but if you think me prudent become as I am, for we ought to imitate what is good. And if I had come to you I should have imitated you; but if you to me, become as I am, for I am a Christian." But they departed with wonder, for they saw that even demons feared Antony.

73. And again others such as these met him in the outer mountain and thought to mock him because he had not learned letters. And Antony said to them, "What do you say? Which is first, mind or letters? And which is the cause of which—mind of letters or letters of mind?" And when they answered mind is first and the inventor of letters, Antony said, "Whoever, therefore, has a sound mind has not need of letters." This answer amazed both the bystanders and the philosophers, and they departed marvelling that they had seen so much understanding in an ignorant man. For his manners were not rough as though he had been reared in the mountain and there grown old, but graceful and polite, and his speech was seasoned with the divine salt, so that no one was envious, but rather all rejoiced over him who visited him.

74. After this again certain others came; and these were men who were deemed wise among the Greeks, and they asked him a reason for our faith in Christ. But when they attempted to dispute concerning the preaching of the divine Cross and meant to mock, Antony stopped for a little, and first pitying their ignorance, said, through an interpreter, who could skilfully interpret his words, "Which is more beautiful, to confess the Cross or to attribute to those whom you call gods adultery and the seduction of boys? For that which is chosen by us is a sign of courage and a sure token of the contempt of death, while yours are the passions of licentiousness. Next, which is better, to say that the Word of God was not changed, but, being the same, He took a human body for the salvation and well-being of man, that having shared in human birth He might make man partake in

the divine and spiritual nature; or to liken the divine to senseless animals and consequently to worship four-footed beasts, creeping things and the likenesses of men? For these things, are the objects of reverence of you wise men. But how do you dare to mock us, who say that Christ has appeared as man, seeing that you, bringing the soul from heaven, assert that it has strayed and fallen from the vault of the sky into body? And would that you had said that it had fallen into human body alone, and not asserted that it passes and changes into four-footed beasts and creeping things. For our faith declares that the coming of Christ was for the salvation of men. But you err because you speak of soul as not generated. And we, considering the power and loving-kindness of Providence, think that the coming of Christ in the flesh was not impossible with God. But you, although calling the soul the likeness of Mind, connect it with falls and feign in your myths that it is changeable, and consequently introduce the idea that Mind itself is changeable by reason of the soul. For whatever is the nature of a likeness, such necessarily is the nature of that of which it is a likeness. But whenever you think such a thought concerning Mind, remember that you blaspheme even the Father of Mind Himself.

75. "But concerning the Cross, which would you say to be the better, to bear it, when a plot is brought about by wicked men, nor to be in fear of death brought about under any form whatever; or to prate about the wanderings of Osiris and Isis, the plots of Typhon, the flight of Cronos, his eating his children and the slaughter of his father. For this is your wisdom. But how, if you mock the Cross, do you not marvel at the resurrection?

For the same men who told us of the latter wrote the former. Or why when you make mention of the Cross are you silent about the dead who were raised, the blind who received their sight, the paralytics who were healed, the lepers who were cleansed, the walking upon the sea, and the rest of the signs and wonders, which show that Christ is no longer a man but God? To me you seem to do yourselves much injustice and not to have carefully read our Scriptures. But read and see that the deeds of Christ prove Him to be God come upon earth for the salvation of men.

76. "But do you tell us your religious beliefs. What can you say of senseless creatures except senselessness and ferocity? But if, as I hear, you wish to say that these things are spoken of by you as legends, and you allegorize the rape of the maiden Persephone of the earth; the lameness of Hephæstus of fire; and allegorize the air as Hera, the sun as Apollo, the moon as Artemis, and the sea as Poseidon; none the less, you do not worship God Himself, but serve the creature rather than God who created all things. For if because creation is beautiful you composed such legends, still it was fitting that you should stop short at admiration and not make gods of the things created; so that you should not give the honour of the Creator to that which is created. Since, if you do, it is time for you to divert the honour of the master builder to the house built by him; and of the general to the soldier. What then can you reply to these things, that we may know whether the Cross has anything worthy of mockery?"

77. But when they were at a loss, turning hither and there, Antony smiled and said—again through an interpreter—"Sight itself carries the conviction of these things. But as you prefer to

lean upon demonstrative arguments, and as you, having this art, wish us also not to worship God, until after such proof, do you tell first how things in general and specially the recognition of God are accurately known. Is it through demonstrative argument or the working of faith? And which is better, faith which comes through the inworking (of God) or demonstration by arguments?" And when they answered that faith which comes through the inworking was better and was accurate knowledge, Antony said, "You have answered well, for faith arises from disposition of soul, but dialectic from the skill of its inventors. Wherefore to those who have the inworking through faith, demonstrative argument is needless, or even superfluous. For what we know through faith this you attempt to prove through words, and often you are not even able to express what we understand. So the inworking through faith is better and stronger than your professional arguments."

78. "We Christians therefore hold the mystery not in the wisdom of Greek arguments, but in the power of faith richly supplied to us by God through Jesus Christ. And to show that this statement is true, behold now, without having learned letters, we believe in God, knowing through His works His providence over all things. And to show that our faith is effective, so now we are supported by faith in Christ, but you by professional logomachies. The portents of the idols among you are being done away, but our faith is extending everywhere. You by your arguments and quibbles have converted none from Christianity to Paganism. We, teaching the faith on Christ, expose your superstition, since all recognise that Christ is God and the Son of God. You by your

eloquence do not hinder the teaching of Christ. But we by the mention of Christ crucified put all demons to flight, whom you fear as if they were gods. Where the sign of the Cross is, magic is weak and witchcraft has no strength.

79. "Tell us therefore where your oracles are now? Where are the charms of the Egyptians? Where the delusions of the magicians? When did all these things cease and grow weak except when the Cross of Christ arose? Is It then a fit subject for mockery, and not rather the things brought to nought by it, and convicted of weakness? For this is a marvellous thing, that your religion was never persecuted, but even was honoured by men in every city, while the followers of Christ are persecuted, and still our side flourishes and multiplies over yours. What is yours, though praised and honoured, perishes, while the faith and teaching of Christ, though mocked by you and often persecuted by kings, has filled the world. For when has the knowledge of God so shone forth? Or when has self-control and the excellence of virginity appeared as now? Or when has death been so despised except when the Cross of Christ has appeared? And this no one doubts when he sees the martyr despising death for the sake of Christ, when he sees for Christ's sake the virgins of the Church keeping themselves pure and undefiled.

How he confuted the philosophers by healing certain vexed with demons

80. "And these signs are sufficient to prove that the faith of Christ alone is the true religion. But see! You still do not believe and are seeking for arguments. We however make our proof 'not in

the persuasive words of Greek wisdom' (1 Corinthians 2:4) as our teacher has it, but we persuade by the faith which manifestly precedes argumentative proof. Behold there are here some vexed with demons;"—now there were certain who had come to him very disquieted by demons, and bringing them into the midst he said—"Do you cleanse them either by arguments and by whatever art or magic you choose, calling upon your idols, or if you are unable, put away your strife with us and you shall see the power of the Cross of Christ." And having said this he called upon Christ, and signed the sufferers two or three times with the sign of the Cross. And immediately the men stood up whole, and in their right mind, and immediately gave thanks unto the Lord. And the philosophers, as they are called, wondered, and were astonished exceedingly at the understanding of the man and at the sign which had been wrought. But Antony said, "Why marvel ye at this? We are not the doers of these things, but it is Christ who works them by means of those who believe in Him. Believe, therefore, also yourselves, and you shall see that with us there is no trick of words, but faith through love which is wrought in us towards Christ; which if you yourselves should obtain you will no longer seek demonstrative arguments, but will consider faith in Christ sufficient." These are the words of Antony. And they marvelling at this also, saluted him and departed, confessing the benefit they had received from him.

How the Emperors wrote to Antony, and of his answer

81. And the fame of Antony came even unto kings. For Constantine Augustus, and his sons Constantius and Constans the Augusti wrote letters to him, as to a father, and begged an answer

from him. But he made nothing very much of the letters, nor did he rejoice at the messages, but was the same as he had been before the Emperors wrote to him. But when they brought him the letters he called the monks and said, "Do not be astonished if an emperor writes to us, for he is a man; but rather wonder that God wrote the Law for men and has spoken to us through His own Son." (Hebrews 1:2.) And so he was unwilling to receive the letters, saying that he did not know how to write an answer to such things. But being urged by the monks because the emperors were Christians, and lest they should take offense on the ground that they had been spurned, he consented that they should be read, and wrote an answer approving them because they worshipped Christ, and giving them counsel on things pertaining to salvation: "not to think much of the present, but rather to remember the judgment that is coming, and to know that Christ alone was the true and Eternal King." He begged them to be merciful and to give heed to justice and the poor. And they having received the answer rejoiced. Thus he was dear to all, and all desired to consider him as a father.

How he saw in a vision the present doings of the Arians

82. Being known to be so great a man, therefore, and having thus given answers to those who visited him, he returned again to the inner mountain, and maintained his wonted discipline. And often when people came to him, as he was sitting or walking, as it is written in Daniel, (Daniel 4:19) he became dumb, and after a season he resumed the thread of what he had been saying before to the brethren who were with him. And his companions perceived that he was seeing a vision. For often when he was

on the mountains he saw what was happening in Egypt, and told it to Serapion the bishop, who was indoors with him, and who saw that Antony was wrapped in a vision. Once as he was sitting and working, he fell, as it were, into a trance, and groaned much at what he saw. Then after a time, having turned to the bystanders with groans and trembling, he prayed, and falling on his knees remained so a long time. And having arisen the old man wept. His companions, therefore, trembling and terrified, desired to learn from him what it was. And they troubled him much, until he was forced to speak. And with many groans he spoke as follows: "O, my children, it were better to die before what has appeared in the vision come to pass." And when again they asked him, having burst into tears, he said, "Wrath is about to seize the Church, and it is on the point of being given up to men who are like senseless beasts. For I saw the table of the Lord's House, and mules standing around it on all sides in a ring, and kicking the things therein, just like a herd kicks when it leaps in confusion. And you saw," said he, "how I groaned, for I heard a voice saying, My altar shall be defiled." These things the old man saw, and after two years the present inroad of the Arians and the plunder of the churches took place, when they violently carried off the vessels, and made the heathen carry them; and when they forced the heathen from the prisons to join in their services, and in their presence did upon the Table as they would. Then we all understood that these kicks of the mules signified to Antony what the Arians, senselessly like beasts, are now doing. But when he saw this vision, he comforted those with him, saying, "Be not downcast, my children; for as the Lord has been angry, so again will He heal us, and the Church shall soon again receive her own order, and shall shine forth as she is wont. And you shall behold the persecuted restored, and wickedness again withdrawn to its own hiding-place, and pious faith speaking boldly in every place with all freedom. Only defile not yourselves with the Arians, for their teaching is not that of the Apostles, but that of demons and their father the devil; yea, rather, it is barren and senseless, and without light understanding, like the senselessness of these mules."

That his healings were done by Christ alone, through prayer

83. Such are the words of Antony, and we ought not to doubt whether such marvels were wrought by the hand of a man. For it is the promise of the Saviour, when He says, "If you have faith as a grain of mustard seed, you shall say to this mountain, remove hence and it shall remove; and nothing shall be impossible unto you." (Matthew 17:20.) And again, "Verily, verily, I say unto you, if you shall ask the father in My name He will give it you. Ask and you shall receive." (John 16:23.) And He himself it is who says to His disciples and to all who believe in Him, "Heal the sick, cast out demons; freely you have received, freely give." (Matthew 10:8.)

84. Antony, at any rate, healed not by commanding, but by prayer and speaking the name of Christ. So that it was clear to all that it was not he himself who worked, but the Lord who showed mercy by his means and healed the sufferers. But Antony's part was only prayer and discipline, for the sake of which he stayed

in the mountain, rejoicing in the contemplation of divine things, but grieving when troubled by much people, and dragged to the outer mountain. For all judges used to ask him to come down, because it was impossible for them to enter on account of their following of litigants. But nevertheless they asked him to come that they might but see him. When therefore he avoided it and refused to go to them, they remained firm, and sent to him all the more the prisoners under charge of soldiers, that on account of these he might come down. Being forced by necessity, and seeing them lamenting, he came into the outer mountain, and again his labour was not unprofitable. For his coming was advantageous and serviceable to many; and he was of profit to the judges, counselling them to prefer justice to all things; to fear God, and to know, "that with what judgment they judged, they should be judged." (Matthew 7:2.) But he loved more than all things his sojourn in the mountain.

How wisely he answered a certain duke

85. At another time, suffering the same compulsion at the hands of them who had need, and after many entreaties from the commander of the soldiers, he came down, and when he had come he spoke to them shortly of the things which make for salvation, and concerning those who wanted him, and was hastening away. But when the duke, as he is called, entreated him to stay, he replied that he could not linger among them, and persuaded him by a pretty simile, saying, "Fishes, if they remain long on dry land, die. And so monks lose their strength if they loiter among you and spend their time with you. Wherefore as fish must hurry to the sea, so must we hasten to the mountain. Lest haply if we

delay we forget the things within us." And the general having heard this and many other things from him, was amazed and said, "Of a truth this man is the servant of God. For, unless he were beloved of God, whence could an ignorant man have such great understanding?"

Of the Duke Balacius, and how, warned by Antony, he met with a miserable end

86. And a certain general, Balacius by name, persecuted us Christians bitterly on account of his regard for the Arians—that name of ill-omen. And as his ruthlessness was so great that he beat virgins, and stripped and scourged monks, Antony at this time wrote a letter as follows, and sent it to him. "I see wrath coming upon you, wherefore cease to persecute the Christians, lest haply wrath catch hold of you, for even now it is on the point of coming upon you." But Balacius laughed and threw the letter on the ground, and spit on it, and insulted the bearers, bidding them tell this to Antony: "Since you take thought for the monks, soon I will come after you also." And five days had not passed before wrath came upon him. For Balacius and Nestorius, the Prefect of Egypt, went forth to the first halting-place from Alexandria, which is called Chæreu, and both were on horseback, and the horses belonged to Balacius, and were the quietest of all his stable. But they had not gone far towards the place when the horses began to frisk with one another as they are wont to do; and suddenly the quieter, on which Nestorius sat, with a bite dismounted Balacius, and attacked him, and tore his thigh so badly with its teeth that he was borne straight back to the city, and in three

days died. And all wondered because what Antony had foretold had been so speedily fulfilled.

How he bore the infirmities of the weak, and of his great benefits to all Egypt

87. Thus, therefore, he warned the cruel. But the rest who came to him he so instructed that they straightway forgot their lawsuits, and felicitated those who were in retirement from the world. And he championed those who were wronged in such a way that you would imagine that he, and not the others, was the sufferer. Further, he was able to be of such use to all, that many soldiers and men who had great possessions laid aside the burdens of life, and became monks for the rest of their days. And it was as if a physician had been given by God to Egypt. For who in grief met Antony and did not return rejoicing? Who came mourning for his dead and did not immediately put off his sorrow? Who came in anger and was not converted to friendship? What poor and low-spirited man met him who, hearing him and looking upon him, did not despise wealth and console himself in his poverty? What monk, having being neglectful, came to him and became not all the stronger? What young man having come to the mountain and seen Antony, did not immediately deny himself pleasure and love temperance? Who when tempted by a demon, came to him and did not find rest? And who came troubled with doubts and did not get quietness of mind?

Of his discernment, and how he was a counsellor to all

88. For this was the wonderful thing in Antony's discipline, that, as I said before, having the gift of discerning spirits, he

recognised their movements, and was not ignorant whither any one of them turned his energy and made his attack. And not only was he not deceived by them himself, but cheering those who were troubled with doubts, he taught them how to defeat their plans, telling them of the weakness and craft of those who possessed them. Thus each one, as though prepared by him for battle, came down from the mountain, braving the designs of the devil and his demons. How many maidens who had suitors, having but seen Antony from afar, remained maidens for Christ's sake. And people came also from foreign parts to him, and like all others, having got some benefit, returned, as though set forward by a father. And certainly when he died, all as having been bereft of a father, consoled themselves solely by their remembrances of him, preserving at the same time his counsel and advice.

How, when now 105 years old, he counselled the monks, and gave advice concerning burial

89. It is worth while that I should relate, and that you, as you wish it, should hear what his death was like. For this end of his is worthy of imitation. According to his custom he visited the monks in the outer mountain, and having learned from Providence that his own end was at hand, he said to the brethren, "This is my last visit to you which I shall make. And I shall be surprised if we see each other again in this life. At length the time of my departure is at hand, for I am near a hundred and five years old." And when they heard it they wept, and embraced, and kissed the old man. But he, as though sailing from a foreign city to his own, spoke joyously, and exhorted them "Not to grow idle in their labours,

nor to become faint in their training, but to live as though dying daily. And as he had said before, zealously to guard the soul from foul thoughts, eagerly to imitate the Saints, and to have nought to do with the Meletian schismatics, for you know their wicked and profane character. Nor have any fellowship with the Arians, for their impiety is clear to all. Nor be disturbed if you see the judges protect them, for it shall cease, and their pomp is mortal and of short duration. Wherefore keep yourselves all the more untainted by them, and observe the traditions of the fathers, and chiefly the holy faith in our Lord Jesus Christ, which you have learned from the Scripture, and of which you have often been put in mind by me."

90. But when the brethren were urging him to abide with them and there to die, he suffered it not for many other reasons, as he showed by keeping silence, and especially for this: The Egyptians are wont to honour with funeral rites, and to wrap in linen cloths at death the bodies of good men, and especially of the holy martyrs; and not to bury them underground, but to place them on couches, and to keep them in their houses, thinking in this to honour the departed. And Antony often urged the bishops to give commandment to the people on this matter. In like manner he taught the laity and reproved the women, saying, "that this thing was neither lawful nor holy at all. For the bodies of the patriarchs and prophets are until now preserved in tombs, and the very body of the Lord was laid in a tomb, and a stone was laid upon it, and hid it until He rose on the third day." And thus saying, he showed that he who did not bury the bodies of the dead after death transgressed the law, even though they were

sacred. For what is greater or more sacred than the body of the Lord? Many therefore having heard, henceforth buried the dead underground, and gave thanks to the Lord that they had been taught rightly.

Of his sickness and his last will

91. But he, knowing the custom, and fearing that his body would be treated this way, hastened, and having bidden farewell to the monks in the outer mountain entered the inner mountain, where he was accustomed to abide. And after a few months he fell sick. Having summoned those who were there—they were two in number who had remained in the mountain fifteen years, practising the discipline and attending on Antony on account of his age—he said to them, "I, as it is written, (Joshua 23:14) go the way of the fathers, for I perceive that I am called by the Lord. And do you be watchful and destroy not your long discipline, but as though now making a beginning, zealously preserve your determination. For you know the treachery of the demons, how fierce they are, but how little power they have. Wherefore fear them not, but rather ever breathe Christ, and trust Him. Live as though dying daily. Give heed to yourselves, and remember the admonition you have heard from me. Have no fellowship with the schismatics, nor any dealings at all with the heretical Arians. For you know how I shunned them on account of their hostility to Christ, and the strange doctrines of their heresy. Therefore be the more earnest always to be followers first of God and then of the Saints; that after death they also may receive you as well-known friends into the eternal habitations. Ponder over these things and think of them, and if you have any care for me and are mindful of

me as of a father, suffer no one to take my body into Egypt, lest haply they place me in the houses, for to avoid this I entered into the mountain and came here. Moreover you know how I always put to rebuke those who had this custom, and exhorted them to cease from it. Bury my body, therefore, and hide it underground yourselves, and let my words be observed by you that no one may know the place but you alone. For at the resurrection of the dead I shall receive it incorruptible from the Saviour. And divide my garments. To Athanasius the bishop give one sheepskin and the garment whereon I am laid, which he himself gave me new, but which with me has grown old. To Serapion the bishop give the other sheepskin, and keep the hair garment yourselves. For the rest fare ye well, my children, for Antony is departing, and is with you no more."

Of Antony's death

92. Having said this, when they had kissed him, he lifted up his feet, and as though he saw friends coming to him and was glad because of them—for as he lay his countenance appeared joyful— he died and was gathered to the fathers. And they afterward, according to his commandment, wrapped him up and buried him, hiding his body underground. And no one knows to this day where it was buried, save those two only. But each of those who received the sheepskin of the blessed Antony and the garment worn by him guards it as a precious treasure. For even to look on them is as it were to behold Antony; and he who is clothed in them seems with joy to bear his admonitions.

How Antony remained hale until his death, and how the fame of him filled all the world

93. This is the end of Antony's life in the body and the above was the beginning of the discipline. Even if this account is small compared with his merit, still from this reflect how great Antony, the man of God, was. Who from his youth to so great an age preserved a uniform zeal for the discipline, and neither through old age was subdued by the desire of costly food, nor through the infirmity of his body changed the fashion of his clothing, nor washed even his feet with water, and yet remained entirely free from harm. For his eyes were undimmed and quite sound and he saw clearly; of his teeth he had not lost one, but they had become worn to the gums through the great age of the old man. He remained strong both in hands and feet; and while all men were using various foods, and washings and various garments, he appeared more cheerful and of greater strength. And the fact that his fame has been blazoned everywhere; that all regard him with wonder, and that those who have never seen him long for him, is clear proof of his virtue and God's love of his soul. For not from writings, nor from worldly wisdom, nor through any art, was Antony renowned, but solely from his piety towards God. That this was the gift of God no one will deny. For from whence into Spain and into Gaul, how into Rome and Africa, was the man heard of who abode hidden in a mountain, unless it was God who makes His own known everywhere, who also promised this to Antony at the beginning? For even if they work secretly, even if they wish to remain in obscurity, yet the Lord shows them as lamps to lighten all, that those who hear may thus know that

the precepts of God are able to make men prosper and thus be zealous in the path of virtue.

The end

94. Read these words, therefore, to the rest of the brethren that they may learn what the life of monks ought to be; and may believe that our Lord and Saviour Jesus Christ glorifies those who glorify Him: and leads those who serve Him unto the end, not only to the kingdom of heaven, but here also—even though they hide themselves and are desirous of withdrawing from the world—makes them illustrious and well known everywhere on account of their virtue and the help they render others. And if need be, read this among the heathen, that even in this way they may learn that our Lord Jesus Christ is not only God and the Son of God, but also that the Christians who truly serve Him and religiously believe in Him, prove, not only that the demons, whom the Greeks themselves think to be gods, are no gods, but also tread them under foot and put them to flight, as deceivers and corrupters of mankind, through Jesus Christ our Lord, to whom be glory for ever and ever. Amen.

Book Catalog

Works by Our Authors

- *The Opium of Happiness* by Jeremy Hausotter. This book examines the Church's teachings on drugs and marijuana. It also contains about 70 pages of appendices of hard to find Church documents discussing drugs. ISBN: 978-1-964170-54-1

- *How to Win Tic Tac Toe Like a Champion* by Jeremy Hausotter. ISBN: 978-1-964170-58-9

Theology & Philosophy

- *Select Works* by **St. Ambrose**. ISBN: 978-1-964170-44-2

- **St. Thomas Aquinas**

    - *The Summa Theologiae: Prima Pars, Q. 1-119.* ISBN: 978-1-964170-23-7

    - *The Summa Theologiae: Prima Secundae, Q. 1-114.* ISBN: 978-1-964170-24-4

    - *The Summa Theologiae: Secunda Secundae, Q. 1-189.* ISBN: 978-1-964170-25-1

    - *The Summa Theologiae: Tertia Pars, Q. 1-90.* ISBN: 978-1-964170-27-5

    - *The Summa Theologiae: Supplementum, Q. 1-99.* ISBN: 978-1-964170-28-2

- *The Life of St. Anthony* by **St. Athanasius**. ISBN: 978-1-964170-20-6

- **St. Augustine**

    - *On Christian Doctrine.* ISBN: 978-1-964170-74-9

    - *Select Doctrinal and Moral Treatises* ISBN: 978-1-964170-63-3

    - *The Anti-Donatist Works.* ISBN: 978-1-964170-40-4

    - *The Anti-Manichean Works.* ISBN: 978-1-964170-67-1

    - *The Anti-Pelagian Works.* ISBN: 978-1-964170-65-7

- *The Art of Dying Well* by **St. Robert Bellarmine**.
  ISBN: 978-1-964170-62-6

- *Select Letters and Orations* by **St. Gregory Nazianzen**.
  ISBN: 978-1-964170-56-5

- **St. John Henry Newman**

  - *An Essay in Aid of a Grammar of Assent.*
    ISBN: 978-1-964170-52-7

  - *The Complete Parochial and Plain Sermons*, volumes 1–4. ISBN:
    978-1-964170-22-0

  - *The Complete Parochial and Plain Sermons*, volumes 5–8. ISBN:
    978-1-964170-66-4

  - *The Complete Historical Sketches*, volumes 1–3.
    ISBN: 978-1-964170-71-8

  - *On the Development of Christian Doctrine.*
    ISBN: 978-1-964170-48-0

  - *Sermons Preached on Various Occasions.*
    ISBN: 978-1-964170-50-3

- *The Problem of Form in Painting and Sculpture* by **Adolf von
  Hildebrand**. ISBN: 978-1-964170-60-2

Papal Documents

- **The Papal Writings of John Paul II**

  - Vol. 1, *The Complete Encyclicals.* ISBN: 978-1-964170-21-3

  - Vol. 2, *Redemptor Hominis.* ISBN: 978-1-964170-00-8

  - Vol. 3, *Dives in Misericordia.* ISBN: 978-1-964170-01-5

  - Vol. 4, *Laborem Exercens.* ISBN: 978-1-964170-02-2

  - Vol. 5, *Slavorum Apostoli.* ISBN: 978-1-964170-03-9

  - Vol. 6, *Dominum et Vivificantem.* ISBN: 978-1-964170-04-6

  - Vol. 7, *Redemptoris Mater.* ISBN: 978-1-964170-05-3

  - Vol. 11, *Veritatis Splendor.* ISBN: 978-1-964170-09-1

  - Vol. 12, *Evangelium Vitae.* ISBN: 978-1-964170-10-7

- Vol. 14, *Fides et Ratio*. ISBN: 978-1-964170-12-1

- **The Papal Writings of Benedict XVI**

    - Vol. 1, *Select Papal Writings: The Encyclicals, Apostolic Exhortations, and Select Other Writings.* ISBN: 978-1-964170-14-5

Classics

- **The Complete Works of Fyodor Dostoevsky**

    - Vol. 8, *The Minor Novels and Novellas: The Insulted and the Injured, The House of the Dead.* ISBN: 978-1-964170-17-6

    - Vol. 9, *The Complete Short Stories.* ISBN: 978-1-964170-18-3

- *The Wind in the Willows* by **Kenneth Grahame**. ISBN: 978-1-964170-46-6

- **Greek and Roman Classics**

    - Vol. 1, *Homer's The Iliad and the Odyssey*, translated by Alexander Pope. ISBN: 978-1-964170-15-2

    - Vol. 4, *Commentaries* by Julius Caesar. ISBN: 978-1-964170-72-5

- **Norse Classics**

    - Vol. 1, *The Poetic and Prose Eddas.* ISBN: 978-1-964170-37-4

    - Vol. 2, *The Heimskringla.* ISBN: 978-1-964170-39-8

    - Vol. 3, *The Nibelungenlied* (prose translation). ISBN: 978-1-964170-33-6

    - Vol. 4, *The Norse Sagas, Part 1.* ISBN: 978-1-964170-35-0

    - Vol. 5, *The Norse Sagas, Part 2.* ISBN: 978-1-964170-29-9

    - Vol. 6, *The Norse Sagas, Part 3.* ISBN: 978-1-964170-31-2

- *20,000 Leagues Under the Sea* by **Jules Verne**. ISBN: 978-1-964170-42-8

Forthcoming Titles

- A volume on the dogma *no salvation outside of the Church* by Jeremy Hausotter.

- A volume on the hermeneutics of Vatican II by Jeremy Hausotter.
- The *Summa Contra Gentiles* by St. Thomas Aquinas.